Quick-Fix Cooking
with
Roadkill

Quick-Fix
Cooking
with

Buck "Buck" Peterson

Illustrated by J. Angus "Sourdough" McLean

**Andrews McMeel
Publishing, LLC**
Kansas City • Sydney • London

Quick-Fix Cooking with Roadkill

10 11 12 13 14 RR2 10 9 8 7 6 5 4 3 2 1

ISBN-13: 978-0-7407-9130-7
ISBN-10: 0-7407-9130-3

Library of Congress Control Number: 2010921937

www.andrewsmcmeel.com
www.buckpeterson.com

ATTENTION: SCHOOLS AND BUSINESSES

Andrews McMeel books are available at quantity discounts with bulk purchase for educational, business, or sales promotional use. For information, please write to: Special Sales Department, Andrews McMeel Publishing, LLC, 1130 Walnut Street, Kansas City, Missouri 64106.

- -

This book contains proprietary, confidential, and/or privileged information that is intended only for use by the individual that paid full price. Those who paid less than full price shall have use of the information in proportion to the final paid price, less sales tax. Those who paid with Canadian dollars have their own national shame to deal with. Readers that purchased this book in a secondhand store are prohibited from the disclosure, copying, or distribution of the contents.

Buck assumes no responsibility for the behavior of any reader and requests that leftovers be donated to your local parish.

- -

J. Angus "Sourdough" McLean

(1941–2010)

BUCK'S BEST PAL AND MASTER ILLUSTRATOR

*The office light in our favorite logger bar
is dimmed in his memory.*

Errata

The publisher and author wish to apologize for the errors that appear in the text. These errors are not their fault. The guilty, once found, will be disciplined behind the woodshed.

Page 22. Buck's Quick Tip: If you prefer habanero peppers to green bell peppers, store toilet paper in the freezer.

Page 25. Bird identification: Male ducks are called drakes because they didn't want to be called hens.

Page 27. There is no good reason to put this sort of information in a book written for the general public. Please disregard.

Pages 28–116. Ditto.

Page 117. Official note from the Bureau of Alcohol, Tobacco, Firearms and Explosives (ATF): Buck does not have a license to sell homemade alcohol at drive-in movies, except in Texas.

Page 118. St. Regis never managed that hotel on 53rd Street. He lost the contract to St. Moritz in a poker game.

Page 119. The Second Vatican Council has ruled that the use of a turkey baster for any purpose other than cooking is one mother of a sin. Penance is twenty Hail Marys and one pound of Stove Top Stuffing®.

Page 122. Official note from ATF: Buck does not have a license to sell homegrown tobacco unless wrapped in a tiny, tubelike paper container.

Page 129. One large Canadian honker poops over 15,000 pounds during its lifetime, even without eating your mother-in-law's meat loaf.

Page 132. Buck's wine-growing region is described as a golden valley, but that doesn't mean his sweet spot is a smoggy suburb of Minneapolis.

Page 135. The male turkey is called a Tom by default. Nobody at the Turkey Tribunal wanted Dick or Harry as the fowl's surname.

Page 138. Wild duck fat cannot be used in general plastic surgery, with the exception of elective gluteoplasty in California.

Page 146. Official note from ATF: Buck does not have a license to sell firearms at the annual Lutefisk dinner at the Sons of Norway Lodge, period.

Page 148. Buck's wine is never described in press quotes as "Two Buck Upchuck." That title belongs to some other Joe.

Page 151. A wine's "nose" can be best enjoyed by a nose free of hair and boogers.

Page 154. Follow-up to official note from AFT re: Buck's licenses. And he never will.

Page 156. "Oh, for the love of Pete," said suddenly single Lena.

Page 157. In a recent study of men wearing sandals to work, the more green tea a man drinks, the less likely he will have a bowel movement while sleeping.

Page 158. Dirty laundry dropped at the back door of the French Laundry in Yountville after nine a.m. will be returned to sender.

Page 159. A message from the American Freezer-Burned Game Meat Institute: "Pfffrrrrrt!" Cosponsored by Industrial-Strength Beano®.

Dedication

Buck dedicates this book to the individuals who have given him hope and inspiration: Rachel Ray, Billy Jean King, Emeril Lagasse, Mortimer Snerd, Bobby Flay, Bluto, Jamie Oliver, Carrot Top, Jim Harrison, Robert Service, Nigella Lawson, Emo Philips, Delia Smith, Enrico Caruso, Mario Batali, Harpo Marx, the Galloping Gourmet, Tom Mix, Gordon Ramsey, the Love Chef, Gallagher, the Love-That-Dare-Not-Speak-Its-Name Chef, Harvey Wallbanger, Mark Miller, Ted Nugent, the Pillsbury Doughboy, Quick-Draw McGraw, the Barefoot Contessa, Aunt Jemima, Julia Child, Uncle Remus, Martha Stewart, Stuart Little, Paula Dean, Mr. Bean, Paul Prudhomme, Tom Collins, Thomas Keller, André the Giant, Mark Bittman, Sgt. Preston, John Wayne, Alice Waters, Screamin' Jay Hawkins, Jacques Pépin, My Friend Flicka, Uncle George, Dorothy the Hunting Pig, and the Executive Staff of the North American Irritable Bowel Institute and 24/7 Rest Stop.

Contents

INTRODUCTION: Life in the High Animal Occupancy Lane, or Dining at the Automat xv

WHAT IS WILD GAME? 1

Wild Game Nutritional Value 3

THE ROAD GROCERY SHOPPER'S TIP SHEET 5

When to Shop, Where to Shop 5

Big Game, Small Game, Birds, Endangered Species, Farm-Fresh Domestic Game, Insects, Vegetables, and Eating Dirt 6

Buck's Famous Deer Camp Fried Squirrel Recipe 12

Special One-Pot Meal: Woking the Dog 15

Beer-Butt Peacock 19

Pheasant Schnitzled. 21

Sweet and Crunchy Insects 30

Corn on the Rob 'er Cob 32

Roasted Road Russets. 33

How to Shop, Essential Gear, Be a Responsible (Green) Roadside Shopper. 35

How to Tell When an Animal Has Given Up the Ghost 43

Methods of Preparation 46

How to Tell When Your Meal Is Ready. 49

Leftovers, or Remains of the Day 51

QUICK-FIX RECIPES ANYONE CAN COOK 53

Deep-Ditch Pizza 54

Freeway Frittata. 55

Croaked Frogs' Legs 57

Grand Slam Burger 58

Grand Slam Sliders 59

The Grateful Dead 61

Shish Kaboom Kebabs 62

Street Meatballs 65

Wrecktangle MeataBall 65

Baby Cracked Ribs. 67

Pavement Panini 68

Tar-Tare. 70

Sunday Family Dinner ("Weekends Are Made for Michelins"):
Mom's Home Cooking 72

Peasant Pheasant Supreme. 73

Neither Hide nor Hair. 74

For the Little Tots 75

Playing with Your Food: Quick-Fix Recipes
for Kids of All Ages. 76

Upland Bird Fingers. 77

Perky Jerky 78

SPECIAL ENTERTAINING OCCASIONS 79

Entertaining with Roadkill 79

All-Purpose Entertaining 82
    The Fondue Party 82

Kentucky Derby 84
    Giddyup Eat-It-Up Steak 85
    Horsemeat with an Asian Flair: Basashi (Sushi) 86

Testicle Festival 87
    Tasty Tidbits from Under a Buck 87

Game Day 90
    Wild Wings 91
    Tailgate Chili 92

HOLIDAYS 93

Groundhog Day 93
    Ground Groundhog 94

Easter 95
    Petered-Out Rabbit 96
    Buck's Welsh Rabbit 98

St. Patrick's Day 99
    Highway Smashed Browns 100
    Corned Carnage and Cabbage 101

Cinco de Mayo 103

    Tex-Mess Taco 105

    Boulevard Burrito 106

    Tarmac Taco Salad. 107

Father's Day. 108

    Road-Salted Rib Eye. 108

Fourth of July 110

    Top Dog. 111

Thanksgiving 113

    Turnkey Turkey 114

Christmas 116

    I'm Dreaming of a Whitetail Christmas 117

ODDS AND ENDS 119

    Buck's Dream Kitchen 119

    A Short Wine Primer: What Every Quick-Fix Chef
    Needs to Know 122

    Offal Things with Recipes 129

    Disclaimers in All North American Languages 135

    Bucket List: One Hundred Animals to Run Over
    Before You Eat a Dirt Sandwich 137

    Roadkill Chefs' Best Cooking Secrets 139

ABOUT THE AUTHOR 141

Life in the High Animal Occupancy Lane, or Dining at the Automat

O ur on-the-go society has required every segment of our consumer culture to accelerate, especially in one of our most basic daily functions—eating. With few exceptions, the pace of private and public dining has gravitated toward fast food, at home and in restaurants. Not only eat-and-run fast food, but fast and easy-to-prepare healthy meals. Celebrity chefs are capitalizing on this need with signature or branded tapas and appetizer "rafts," easy/fast cookbooks, and demonstrations on Food Network shows. Another sustainable trend that has recently appeared is the interest in "natural" or "organic" foodstuffs. Although the term *organic* has different meanings in different settings, there can be no question that consumers, in particular new parents, want to serve food that is qualifiably less processed and less modified than their parents did. Grandparents who want visiting privileges have also jumped on this food cart.

Experts predict that the shakedowns from an artificially robust national and global economy will alter our behavior forever. People eat more at home now, with the renewed family values of healthy meals. People cook more, relearning portion sizes and reading nutritional data. Families spend less and save more, and grow their own vegetables. Coupon clipping has returned to the middle class. And taste reigns supreme in the modern kitchen. Taste, in most minds, is a four-pack—salty, bitter, sweet, and sour—but the Japanese have introduced a fifth that fits road food to a T. *Umami,* Japanese for "deliciousness," is described as "food with attitude," and any culture that produces the Toyota Land Cruiser shopping cart has an open lane on Buck's highway. P.S. Roadkill is food you can see in the dark.

A CORNUCOPIA OF REASONS FOR
A ROADKILL FOOD REGIMEN

- Roadkill is sustainable. As we continue to squeeze animal populations into tighter areas, the supermarket always has a full meat case. Even commercially raised meat has similar space issues: Chickens at the largest producers are so squeezed that reports of long eggs with pointed ends are surfacing. Turkeys are packed in long sheds and don't have room to lift their legs to take a leak, and pigs are left without enough room to be huffed and puffed down.

- Roadkill shopping provides the opportunity for unscheduled exercise (sometimes they don't lie down right away). This reduces stress (depending on how close the game warden is following), stretches your legs (depending on the speed of the species), and lowers blood pressure (depending on how heavy an animal is to stuff in your trunk).

- In most cases, roadkill is wild game, and wild game flavors are unique—no need for a food snot's expensive special spices. Wild game can rarely be prepared wrong, and if it does taste funny to those with nature-deficiency disorders, blame it on the animal. For easy preparation, there is no need to bring freeway-aged wild game meat to room temperature.

- Roadkill is good for all ages. It teaches children not to run in the street, chase a ball between parked cars, and, more important, not take candy from Republicans running for reelection. Seniors love roadkill because, in most cases, the food is warm and soft and reduces the need for stool-softeners.

- Roadkill shopping always has an element of surprise in a world of even more predictability. On the road, you never know what you will run into. Who's coming home for dinner? Who cares! No endless worry about menu planning.

- Roadkill, best of all, provides the fresh opportunity to eat alone, without friends, family, and other codependents.

Let's get to the meat of the matter. This is, after all, a meat cookbook and as one sympathetic wag put it, if we weren't meant to eat animals, then why are they made out of meat? Quick-Fix recipes come in two versions: very fast, on the go and those that take longer preparation for fast later use. The simple high-fiber recipes are designed to make you healthy. In a two-day, one-night clinical study at the College of the Great Loon Spirit in northern Minnesota just outside of Nevis, home of the Great Northern Pike, Quick-Fix Program participants lost an average of 3 ounces, lowered their blood sugar level by 2 cups, and had less painful bowel movements than those in a poorly run rest home protocol.

Quick-Fix recipes are designed to be quick so you can spend valuable time doing other things, such as tanning hides and making jewelry of animal claws and evening purses from bull nut-sacks. Some recipes are quick to make and then frozen for "warm-ups" later.

The careful reader will notice that no advertisers are buying brand identity through product placement in this book. Somewhere, honest and unbiased and qualified opinion must rule.

These easy recipes are perfect for these economic times. Those who avoid the fare produced by commercial kitchens by cooking more at home are known to eat less, and eating wild animals that would otherwise go to waste is a very economical choice. The case can be made that eating roadkill will lead to world peace, except in Wisconsin.

You're welcome. God bless you and God bless northern Minnesota.

BUCK "BUCK" PETERSON,
Executive Director, Meals Under Wheels Foundation

Publisher's Note: Gourmands that expect the ingredients of a recipe to harmonize with one another much like a husband and wife will find no solace here. Given Buck's marital record, it's no wonder his recipes are chaotic.

What Is Wild Game?

Wild game is not an animal raised or managed by private individuals or corporations, and not the game meat sold by restaurants and other public food outlets. Much of the commercial red meat is farmed in New Zealand; their venison and lamb is considered top-notch by the field handicapped, but still not wild. But Buck is wild about their fine wool long johns that don't make you itch.

Wild game is wild meat, unlike the domestic meat found in refrigerated cases at the supermarket. Marketers for the industrial farms don't mention the genetic altering required to produce the big-breasted chickens that produce chicken backaches. Cows don't have bright white teeth so in fashion with TV talking heads, and don't enjoy the crowding in feedlots. If you could ask them how things are going, they'd tell you. The most insidious image manipulation is with organic dairy cattle that clearly show the use of Botox to present the happiest visage to Whole Earth shoppers.

Wild game is Mother Nature's healthiest meat. Wild animals eat organic fruits and vegetables and pass the nutrition on to you. For example, whitetail deer, the wild game species with the largest availability of fresh meat, eat acorns, corn, apples, leaves of your saplings, and grasses. They particularly like the produce section of a golf course, with the notable exception of areas used by elderly golfers with bladder issues.

Wild game is not likely to suffer from the diseases of domestic herd animals and flocks. Cow elk, for example, do not carry mad cow disease but get as upset as an elk can be when you break up their immediate family group. Pheasants can't transmit hoof-and-mouth disease; they have no hooves and just a beak for a mouth.

Wild game tastes different than domestic animals. Domestic animal meat is easier to describe: red meat, white meat, the other white meat, and nicely marbled barn cat meat from a dairy farm. Wild game has similar categories, but each animal has a special flavor. Antelope, for example, has a rather sweet taste, whereas raccoon meat has a finish that smacks of Purina Cat Chow®. Each flavor is conditioned by the animal's diet and means of acquisition. The meat of a whitetail deer living on corn is preferred over that of a sea duck feasting on cruise boat garbage. A coyote purchased after a long, bumpy chase across a wheat field in a Ford pickup truck is stronger flavored than a hobby farmer's pet swan.

Eating venison every day may not enable you to run fast when the man sets a forest fire, but medical evidence points to glossier hair and a slightly larger nut-sack in late October. Wild male birds are not henpecked and migratory birds don't spread exotic diseases, unless you count the Canadian passion for maple sugar. Across the board, wild game has flavors born of unaltered genetics and their habits in the field, not from an artificial diet of species-specific food pellets.

You can use wild game in your favorite family recipes. Replace an equal amount of dove meat instead of chicken for your own Croak au Vin, or road ground round in the meat-and-noodles hot dish destined for the church bazaar. Create an elegant Pot-au-Phew with a fresh skunk top blade roast, or bring a standing rib rump roast of possum to her parents' house to answer their call for something different. The possibilities are endless.

If for no other reason, wild game is better for you and your loved ones.

WILD GAME NUTRITIONAL VALUE

Sampling of Raw Meat, 100 Grams or 3.5 Ounces

	Fat (g)	Cholesterol (mg)	Calories
USDA Beef (standard)	2.7	69	158
Beef (choice)	6.5	72	180
Whitetail Deer	1.4	113	153

Analysis: The better domestic beef you buy, the sooner you will be a candidate for a lard-ass weight-loss program. You can eat twice as much wild game over the same period of time and relieve any chronic constipation.

	Fat (g)	Cholesterol (mg)	Calories
Pork (domestic)	4.9	71	165
Squirrel (wild)	3.2	83	149

Analysis: This clearly demonstrates why squirrel meat is the healthy choice over ham with your morning Grand Slam Bam® breakfast, not to mention substantial saving in birdseed.

Moose meat has the lowest fat content (0.5 g) and cholesterol count (71 mg) among the big boys, and wild pheasants lead the prairie birds with 0.6 g fat and only 52 mg cholesterol. Need Buck say more? Boys and girls, start your engines! Maine for moose, South Dakota for pheasant. Happy motoring, er, shopping.

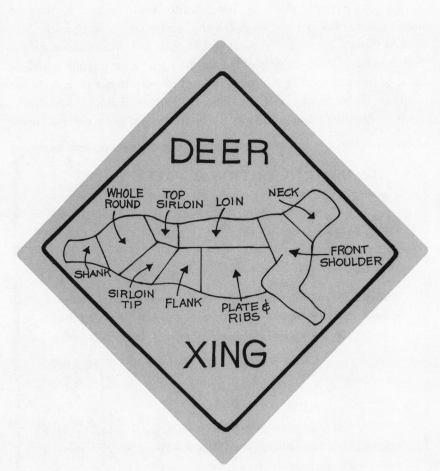

The Road Grocery Shopper's Tip Sheet

When to Shop, Where to Shop

WHEN TO SHOP

- In the spring, when animals are shaking off their long winter naps

- In the summer, when animal schools are closed for the season

- In the fall, when attention turns to romance and animal sports

- In the winter, when it's easier for animals to walk on plowed roads

- During any open hunting season and when hikers, horseback riders, mountain bikers, and nature lovers take to the field

- Especially when Farmer Brown is knocking down that last patch of cornfield

WHERE TO SHOP

- Near where PETA meeting notices are posted

- Near posted farmland and other NO HUNTING, NO FIREARMS signs

- Near long skid marks on the highway

- Near feathers all over the road

- Near game refuges, preserves, hunting clubs, and petting zoos

- Near any water source and cultivated crops, especially grain fields

- And wherever the deer xing sign is displayed

Big Game, Small Game, Birds, Endangered Species, Farm-Fresh Domestic Game, Insects, Vegetables, and Eating Dirt

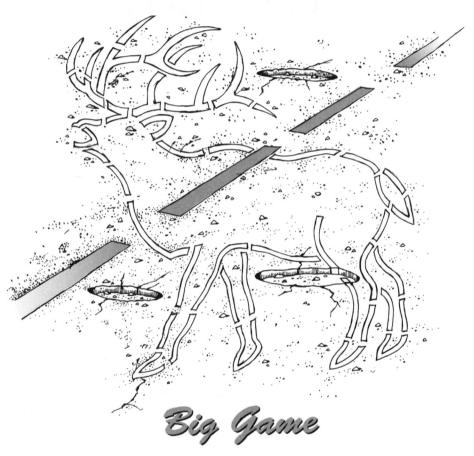

Big Game

Big-game animals are mammals that states charge large fees to hunt. Look for those critters whose game trail crosses yours. Be aware when you plan a large roadside purchase to fill the freezer for the long winter ahead. The meat choices are many and each animal presents its own set of challenges.

ANTELOPE

This fast-moving member of the goat family is unlikely to cross your path during hunting season, as it knows that loud noises during the early fall can cause severe joint pain and soft-tissue loss. However, in the off-season, antelopes like to play animal games in the ditches, especially in the soft light of dawn and dusk, and the opportunity to join in their games is very high.

BEAR

The black and the brown bear rule the food chain. The smaller black bear is not uncommon, especially if you include the federal fire patrol. The brown bear, or grizzly, is rarely encountered on the road. A bear prefers drivers to leave the safety of their car, to rip their face off and eat their young. Smacking a bear is like trying to tip over a big feral hog. The most frequent comment about bear meat, no matter what season, is, "It's not bad." Undercooked bear meat can lead to trichinosis, a parasitic disease that can kill if untreated, to the great delight of the surviving bear family members.

BUFFALO

The North American bison is seldom free-range unless you are in a federal or state park/preserve or on a private ranch. The high value placed on these four-legged meat lockers makes them an unlikely purchase, especially during daylight hours. Most especially in Yellowstone National Park. Compared to beef, buffalo has very low fat and cholesterol content, and too many, including the author, compare it favorably to moose meat. Given the large size and body weight of an adult bison, the premium position in a bison-automobile interaction is the secondary position. Bobby Flay's choice of topping: soft goat cheese.

DEER

Whitetail deer provide the most popular road meat in the country, with mule deer a distant second. Deer meat, or venison, makes you strong and, in large quantities, fleet of foot and able to clear high barbed-wire fences without hip boots. This royal meat is often served in holiday settings (see Christmas, page 116).

In the mid-1700s, a deer hide weighing 2½ pounds was sent to England. This became codpieces and condoms for the royal family, and was valued at forty cents a pound, or a "buck's worth."

ELK

There are two species, the Rocky Mountain elk and the Roosevelt, the larger of the two animals. In Buck's experience, a roadside shopper is more likely to encounter an elk herd crossing the road than a single animal except during the rut. A companion shopper yelping a cow call on the side of the road opposite all the bull bugling should do the trick. Preferred call: anything Primos® makes.

Elk antlers in early velvet are thought to have sexual restorative powers and, once ground into a powder, are sold in apothecaries throughout the Far East and, with the password "Ben Franklin," in Asian communities across America. Other anecdotal benefits: enhances the immune system, reduces symptoms of arthritis, slows the aging process, and lowers LDL (bad) cholesterol. Dogs with ED in particular benefit from a daily dose of 50 mg capsules, with the caveat that your terrier is already humping your arm too often.

Elk also carry a set of ivory in their dentures to commemorate your successful purchase, and can be traded for a double bourbon at most Elk Lodges, especially when the bartender isn't watching.

MOOSE

This is the largest purchase for most road shoppers. With bulls weighing well over a ton, a full-grown North American moose in the freezer will serve a family for a full winter. The moose is the goofiest-looking large game mammal on the roads through low-lying marshlands, and a gentle vegetarian with poor eyesight and a high-strung nervous system. Alaska is the best place to shop for moose meat, where the highway patrol keeps a moose roadkill wish list for residents.

Buck's Quick Tip: Quarter the animal with a chain saw for speedy removal.

General Preparation for Big Game

ROAST

Old-timers salt and pepper large meat chunks in a cast-iron Dutch oven, add water to half-full, throw in sliced onions and other vegetables, and bake at 275°F for about 2 hours per pound.

STEAK (MINUTE)

Cut half-inch steaks and sear for 30 seconds on both sides, season to taste, and serve.

STEAK

Cut inch-and-a-half steaks and sear for 3 minutes on each side. Let the meat rest for 5 minutes before serving.

Buck's Quick Tip: Remove the silver "skin" that wraps muscle groups before cutting steaks.

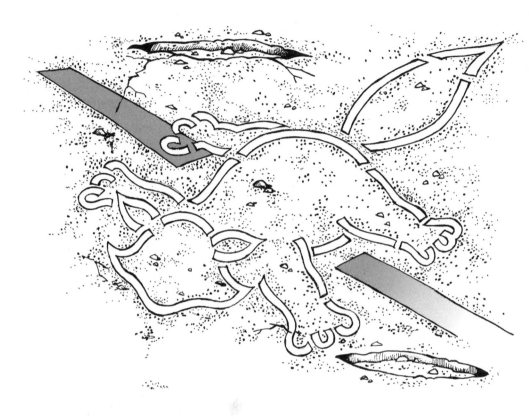

Small Game

As defined by the game and fish departments, small game is everything that's not large game. Because of the smaller size and larger populations, small game offers more opportunities for the roadside shopper. To build a little familiarity, here is a review of the small-game meat counter for the most common daily specials.

POSSUM

For an animal cursed to be born dead by the side of the road, possum recipes are common in their most populous areas, particularly in the South. A marsupial with distant cousins (kangaroo, koala bears, human circus freaks), the nocturnal possum avoids danger by playing possum on the road when the town drunks are weaving their way home. If moose did this, Buck would need another freezer.

RACCOON

The masked bandits have invaded suburbia, gorging on domestic pet chow on the back decks. Coonskin can stretch to unimaginable limits—much like your brother-in-law down in the game room—and these late-night feeders are, in most situations, an easy acquisition. Buck rolled over a big one on a late-night food run, and the old boy just shook it off and waddled back to the deck food near the nineteenth hole. Serving suggestion: Roast raccoon is a dramatic treat when served sitting on its haunches begging for a handout.

SQUIRREL

Best taken in the fall when their family responsibilities are discharged and under a talent contract to a large insurance company, gray squirrels are the most common and larger of the North American squirrel family and an easy pick-me-up on weekend drives in the country, especially when leaf-drinking through the brilliant fall colors. Like its buddies flying above and in a burrow below, a squirrel is easy to prepare. Skin the little bugger by inserting a blade just under the skin, tip up, above its bunghole and cut to the throat, being careful not to nick the meat. Once this is done, grab both sides of its coat and pull backward until it hangs up on its legs, tail, and head. Cut them off. Now remove the plumbing with an incision the full length of its belly, knife tip up, and pull the innards outward. Wash and dry. Put the head on a garden stake next to your bird feeder.

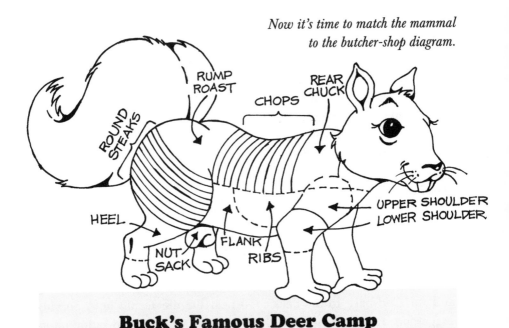

Now it's time to match the mammal to the butcher-shop diagram.

RUMP ROAST

CHOPS

REAR CHUCK

ROUND STEAKS

UPPER SHOULDER

LOWER SHOULDER

HEEL

NUT SACK

FLANK

RIBS

Buck's Famous Deer Camp Fried Squirrel Recipe

Larger squirrel parts, legs, and hams

2 cups buttermilk

¼ cup extra-virgin olive oil

1 cup seasoned all-purpose flour

Salt and ground black pepper

Place the squirrel parts in a glass container and cover with the buttermilk. Store in the refrigerator and let soak overnight. Pat dry and place in a cooler for the drive to deer camp. On arrival, declare dibs on the best bedding by putting used long johns and wool socks on the pillow. Unpack your cooking gear and have a glass of Buck's house wine (see page 126). Heat a cast-iron skillet to medium-high. Roll the squirrel parts in olive oil and then in the seasoned flour. Fry until golden brown, add salt and pepper to taste, and serve on a bed of wild rice with fresh acorns as decoration. Serves two.

Special-Occasion Small Game

BADGER

The badger is a rare ditch-hiker and has a symbiotic relationship with the coyote, often sharing a hole in the ground. This living arrangement makes both very ornery. The structure of badger jaw ensures a firm, almost unbreakable bite, so men should not use a badger hole as a place to go number two. Historical note: Dachshunds were originally used to hunt badgers. This accounts for their warm, gentle demeanor.

BEAVER, MUSKRAT, NUTRIA

Marsh mammals, except for nutria moving north, are rarely found crossing a road unless the beaver needs more dam supplies. These vegetarians are best known for other than culinary excellence: the beaver for 4X cowboy hats, muskrat for the ramble, and nutria for its belly fur in eastern Europe. Trappers with a commitment to recycling will deep-fry marsh mammals, or privately admit to a preference for a sauté in white wine, soy sauce, butter, and garlic. Paul Prudhomme has found uses for nutria in his kitchen, which just goes to show you the lengths coonasses will go to save their dikes. Suggested use: stew meat.

CATS

The three wild cats native to North America in likelihood of appearance in the supermarket are the bobcat, the puma (a.k.a. cougar, panther, or mountain lion), and the Canadian lynx. The puma is commonly spotted in the suburbs where pets raised on the Disney Channel play down by the artificial lake. The Florida panther is an endangered, inbred mixed breed and highly protected. If an interaction occurs, don't stop. Those caught will be guest grub at the nearest alligator farm.

The cats most shoppers are apt to and would like to run into are domestic. There is some confusion in polite circles as to whether this is a good thing, but if you see a black cat crossing your path, ensure that it's the critter's last catwalk. Any unfortunate accident will bring you good luck. Serving suggestion: a short-sided black serving pan with nonscented litter. Garnish with fresh catnip.

DOGS

The meat-eating canine, the dog-eat-dog food chain: wolf, coyote, and fox are all magnificent furbearers in season. And territorial. If you see wolves, you won't see coyotes; if you see coyotes, you won't see foxes. Everyone, including the skunk, is an upland bird and egg eater that deserves a reminder of who rules on the nation's byways.

Wolves never sport a collar with owner ID. If your purchase is wearing a game department tracking collar, remove and hook under your neighbor's car. Suggested use: stew meat.

Buck's Quick Tip: Wolf tastes much like coyote, yet with a hint of elk calf. Coyote tastes like fox with subtle overtones of baby lambs, Peter Rabbit, and Garfield the Cat. Fox tastes like field mice and it takes about forty red fox pelts to make a king-size quilt.

PORCUPINE

These shy north-woods denizens don't care what the chicken sees on the other side of the road and are rarely found near the centerline. Porky is best known for its role in training dogs to keep their noses out of its business, but if shopped can provide a hot, albeit, greasy meal. There is no good reason to save the fat that cocoons this vegetarian's meat. Suggested use: stew meat.

If the animal has not been damaged beyond repair, gut it, wash it in the stream, bag it, and take it to a taxidermist who can make a great party platform for hors d'oeuvres. Thread the quills with cheeses, olives, and pork and pineapple chunks. Tell the taxidermist you want a big smile on the porcupine's face.

Special One-Pot Meal:
Woking the Dog

A simple wok is the perfect cooking vessel for families on the go.
Used woks can be found at secondhand stores and new ones won't
break the bank. Preferred: a wok with handles that stay cool.

4 tablespoons extra-virgin olive oil

**1 pound clean dog meat (the amount found on
an adult Chihuahua) cut into 1½-inch chunks**

12 ounces white mushrooms, sliced

2 cups fresh corn kernels

Heat the oil in a wok over medium-high heat. Add "Pepe" and
sauté (or wok) the dog for 6 minutes, or until browned. Add the
mushrooms and continue to sauté for another 5 minutes. Add
the corn and sauté for several more minutes. Remove from the
heat and serve on a bed of noodles. Send a thank-you note to
PETA. Serves four.

SKUNK

These upland bird egg–sucking garbage bags have one saving grace–a pelt that makes a great winter hat. Skunks are more like a dog in that, when raised from birth, they can be trained to be a pet sensation at the mall. If you insist, remove the small scent glands by the tail to avoid *la phew*. Suggested use: stew for her or his family reunion.

WOODCHUCK

This groundhog is a celebrity animal and the largest of the ground squirrel family. A woodchuck can weigh up to 30 pounds and is the only one that knows the answer to "How much would a woodchuck upchuck if a woodchuck can't read the DO NOT WALK warning sign?" Suggested use: more stew meat.

WOLVERINE

The Finnish national mammal (for its even temper and gregarious nature) is rarely seen in the woods and even more rarely seen crossing a road. The most likely place to see a wolverine is at the movies, and not very good ones at that.

General Preparation for Small Game

MAMMAL-SICLE, OR ANIMAL ON A STICK

Skin, gut, and clean the animal, put on a stick, and roast over an open fire. For dream-free sleeping, have the head or where the head was pointed away from you.

SHISH KABOOM KEBABS (SEE PAGE 62)

Cube the daily special, thread on skewers, and add available fruit and vegetable chunks.

STEW

Game-meat stews are easy and they go like this: Cut the meat into small pieces, brown, and add sliced carrots, onions, celery, russet potatoes, garlic, and red wine. Reduce the wine over medium-high heat, add tomatoes, water, and a bay leaf, then simmer over low heat for a long time, especially when using older animals. Serve when done. You can also put parts in boiling water, lower the heat, and simmer until the meat falls from the bones. Remove the meat and add chopped onions, a can of corn kernels (drained), a large can of chopped tomatoes, a box of frozen peas or lima beans (no WWI C-rations), and bring to a boil, lower the heat, and simmer for 45 minutes. Add the meat back to the pot and simmer for another 30 minutes, stirring as you go. Add water if the stew is too thick; add flour if it is too thin. There you have it. Bon appétit.

The French learned long ago that the right sauce can hide a multitude of culinary sins, not to mention the other sins they're responsible for. The perfect sauce to hide the errors of your way is *au poivre*, from the ancient French word *poivre-sacre-bleu-cheese-flatulent-frog-breath*, which means different things to different people, except for the Germans, who take it as an invitation to invade at their leisure.

Buck's Quick Tips: Brown the meat in bacon grease, add flour and mushrooms, and it starts to look like bourguignon.

Prepare the stew without the road meat so all you have to do is add purchases to complete the preparation. You won't stew about anything if you have this trick in your trunk. Shortcut: Buy a can of ready-made stew at the market, remove the meat, and replace with your browned road meat.

Mashed potatoes or dumplings will cover any errors in the stew pot.

Birds

Birds of a feather flock together, so a bird in the hand is not worth two in the bush when you are on bush-league autopilot!

PEACOCK

The peacock is one of the few birdbrains in Mother Nature's aviary that deserve extinction. Feral peacocks are found near petting zoos, daft households, and hobby farms that once thought the birds of many colors were pretty until the dumb bird ate their vegetables and rose bushes and cawed on the rooftops just when alpha sleep kicked in. Hang your rare purchase on a post or clothesline for several days to show peacock family survivors a vision of their tomorrow. Prepare like a pheasant (the meat's color and flavor are similar) and roast in a large oven, or take inordinate pleasure in preparing this recipe.

Beer-Butt Peacock

1 whole peacock, dressed, cleaned, and dried

6 tablespoons Tony Chachere's® Creole Seasoning or Cavender's® All Purpose Greek Seasoning, or dry barbecue rub of your choice

1 largest beer can you can find, minimum 16 ounces, small keg if possible

2 cups presoaked mesquite chips

Put display feathers inside your favorite beer-branded headband. Apply the rub throughout the peacock body. Prepare the grill for indirect medium heat, with a drip pan. Use a church key to open six holes along the top of the can. Pour off an inch or so of the beer and add a pinch of rub to the remainder. Shove the can up the peacock's butt as high as its voice box and with as much gusto as you can muster. This part of the procedure is extremely gratifying and can be enjoyed even more when the noisy, dirty, thieving bastard is still alive. When your ceremonial dance is complete and your supply of bottle rockets is exhausted, place half of the chips on the fire and stand the big dumb bird with the can up its butt in the center of the grill, over the drip pan. Cover and cook for 3 to 4 hours, adding coals, firewood, and the remaining chips as needed until the meat

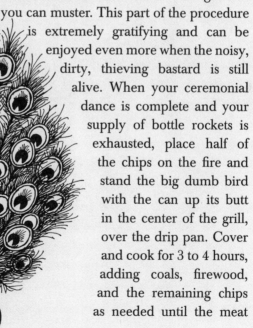

falls off the bone. Remove the bird from the grill and carve away. Serves six.

VARIATION: Preheat the oven to 400°F. Rub the inside of the peacock with garlic-infused extra-virgin olive oil. Mix together 3 cups of bread crumbs, 6 eggs, 1½ teaspoons of ground allspice, 1½ cups of milk, and 3 cups of unpopped popping corn. Stuff the mixture into the cavity and place the peacock in a baking pan. Cover with aluminum foil and bake with the cavity facing the door. Baste frequently while standing carefully to the side. The peacock is done when the popcorn blows its ass out the door.

RING-NECKED PHEASANT

The major bush-league road bird is the ring-necked pheasant. Introduced in 1877, this fat bird is the most popular upland game bird in the United States. The largest ring-neck meat counter is in South Dakota (numbering in the millions), and if you can't purchase a family-size banquet of these tasty cacklers (and state bird) on a county road in "So Dak," your driver's license should be revoked. The legal daily game bag in South Dakota and most neighboring states is three roosters per person. The regulations aren't clear on the limits of road-harvested wrung-necks; to avoid confusion, any extra road birds should be stashed in the trunk until they make up their mind. To avoid suspicion, the Meals Under Wheels Foundation recommends not wearing blaze orange apparel while road shopping during the fall hunting season.

Pheasant Schnitzled

1 cup extra-virgin olive oil

1 large pheasant breast

Bacon-infused salt and ground black pepper

½ cup all-purpose flour

2 eggs, beaten

**½ cup panko (alternatives: crushed Tim's
Cascade Lightly Salted Potato Chips or
French's® French Fried Onions)**

Browned butter

In a skillet, heat the oil over medium-high heat. Pound the breast to ¼ inch thickness if your Goodyears didn't. Season the breast with salt and pepper to taste and roll in the flour. Dip in the beaten eggs and roll in the panko. Fry in the skillet until golden brown. Alternatively, bake for 20 minutes in an oven preheated to 400°F. Remove the breast from the pan, cover with butter, and serve. Serves one.

Buck's Quick Tip: A male pheasant, or cock, will typically breed a dozen or so hens a year. Male peasants exhibit similar behavior.

The official state bird of North Dakota is the western meadowlark, which tells you what they like to shoot there (substitute this bird in any Four-and-Twenty Blackbirds Baked in a Pie recipe). Due to the large number of nonresident shooters attracted to the grasslands of the Midwest, the most popular wild game bird in North Dakota is the South Dakota wounded ring-neck.

If you have the time, roast a whole bird like a turkey and serve when the juices run clear.

If the breasts haven't been reduced to cutlets, pheasant saltimbocca is superb. Pheasant can also be substituted for any recipe using skinless, boneless, tasteless chicken, especially with the skin on.

WILD DUCK

Great timing and discipline is required to shop a wild duck, unless you include the park ducks full of bread crusts, a mallard family trying to cross busy Beacon Street to Boston's Public Garden, or within reach of a Peabody Hotel duck. For many, wild duck meat is an acquired taste. The bold flavor can be muted by an overnight salted water or milk marinade, but Buck prefers to pan-fry the breasts skin on and in butter like a steak, and use a dark berry preserve for the sauce. Roast small wood ducks or early-season teal by leaving the skin on, wrap in apple-wood smoked bacon, and turn over an open fire in aluminum foil until done. Serve over their favorite food, wild rice. Do not serve wild duck to a first date, especially to a city girl embarrassed by body noises, especially her own. Frrrt!

The only duck soup worthy of attention is the movie made by the Marx Brothers.

Save any severely broken bird for dog training. Dress and store in the freezer until use in the field.

WILD GAME BIRDS

Wild game birds present a wide opportunity for the roadside shopper, and there are few areas in our country where they can't be found. Wild game birds can be divided between upland birds and migratory birds. The former are localized populations of tasty light-colored meat birds such as grouse, pheasant, woodcock, partridge, dove, and quail. The latter include flight birds that migrate great distances, such as ducks, geese, swans, and cranes, and are hard to run over unless they are refueling on the ground—with the exception of Canadian geese that prefer safe, secure suburban and golf course living.

The game departments of the states of residence manage upland birds, and the federal government manages migratory birds, especially those crossing the border at night. The game departments and federal government set wild game bird bag limits for hunters, but a road shopper's limit stretches the imagination, along with the game bag when no one in an official capacity is watching.

Here's a sample wild bird scenario: You're driving down a dusty road near Big Bird, South Dakota, and the pickup ahead unknowingly swats a rooster trying to escape the No. 4 lead shot in the food plot. You slide up to the flopping bird, open your car door, grab the bird by the neck, and dispatch and flip the bird in the back while hoping to miss Junior in the baby seat. At the next irrigation ditch, you run a knife from stem to stern, pull the skin back, and in the warm environment wrap your fingers around the breast meat, carefully remove it from the chest cavity, and wash it. If you have a book of matches and dry wood, lunch is served.

A Bye-Bye Birdie breakfast, lunch, and dinner on-the-go is easy, given the wide variety of wild game birds. Upland birds have a wide variety of habitats and preparations are simple to learn. The few questions remaining are: Should I eat there or elsewhere? (Think law enforcement.) Should I eat the best part or the whole bird? What spare parts should I leave on my in-laws' front steps?

Once cleaned or dressed, small birds are roasted on a stick and large birds have the breast meat removed for frying on the manifold when you cook outdoors "on the fly." When food snots talk about dressing wild game birds, they do not put funny clothes on the bird even though they're wearing funny clothes at the time. Dressing birds means removing what you don't want to eat. Feathers are hard to pass without a good stool softener.

For a more gamey taste of your purchase, hang unplucked, undressed birds upside down in a cool environment (refrigerator) for ten days to capture the true flavor of that particular bird. Bachelors are particularly adept at this preparation.

Time dictates the part you eat. With few exceptions, every part of an upland bird is good to eat. Breast out the small birds such as doves and quail and wrap the tender vittles around a chile pepper before putting on a stick. Larger upland birds are roasted whole with the skin on (see Beer-Butt Peacock, page 19) and park swans are baked as far from law enforcement as possible. Sage grouse should only be served at in-law family reunions.

As far as spare parts go, your in-laws' front lawn will look like Freddy Krueger's aviary if done right. Happy Halloween.

Endangered Species

If you are an active roadside shopper, the odds of acquiring an animal on the endangered species list are small but possible. Federal law protects members of an endangered species and travelers intentionally harming (taking) them will face stiff penalties, including a long stretch in the pokey. The long-term residents there have equally bad intentions and will want to play "pokey" with you.

Here are the most likely endangered species you will encounter along our nation's highways:

FLORIDA KEY DEER

Local recovery experts top off a Key deer roast with a slice of Key lime pie. The back straps on these charismatic mega-fauna are small and any recipe should be doubled for adults.

FLORIDA PANTHER

This troubled swamp cat comes with heavy penalties for a cat-car interaction. If a badge witnesses you taking a Florida panther, try to resuscitate the injured ward of the state. Since the mouth is so long, it may be more useful to blow through its nose while pushing the chest bone. Warning: Do not inhale cat breath. The experience will scar you for life.

RED WOLF

The red wolf is most likely to be spotted in North Carolina, where the U.S. Fish and Wildlife Service has established an experimental population without coyote pressure, for a more diverse mixed grill for state residents.

Buck's Quick Tips: The important word in the federal statutes is "intentionally." If a badge can document your tire marks swerving off road to hit an endangered animal, it's time to tell your children you are going on a long vacation.

If you're so hungry that you skinned and ate the fillets of the animal, and your legal defense was your involuntary actions scared the wolf out of its skin, it's another occasion to tell your children you are going on a long vacation and to mind Mom until you get back.

Just because an animal is pronounced endangered by a well-fed Washington bureaucrat doesn't mean it isn't good eating. It just means the government doesn't want to share the culinary enjoyment found in federal recovery rooms.

The giddy sense of accomplishment when taking an endangered animal in the early morning or evening light cannot be underestimated. This is especially true for those from a dysfunctional family that has "You're not supposed to do that" as its motto.

Pride is a sin. The hides, horns, and full-body mounts of endangered species should be stored at your in-laws for their enjoyment, too.

Migrating snowbirds are not an endangered species in Florida. They are not even a threatened species. The best place to encounter them is at the slow-moving snowbird crosswalks.

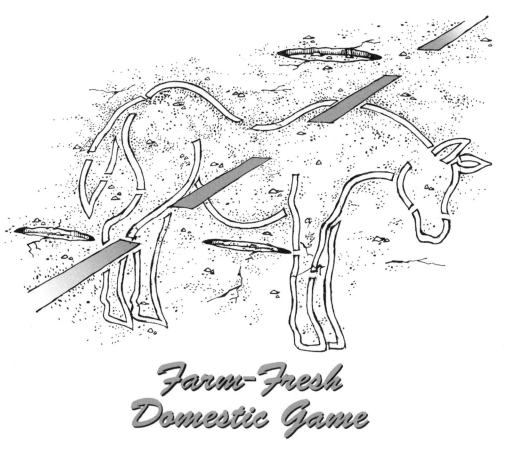

Farm-Fresh Domestic Game

Access to wild game is limited for many urban shoppers. Once free of city boundaries, the next layer of civilization is suburbia, where pickings are slim except for coyotes and a few nondomesticated cats. The closest market with any real selection is the next ring of human habitat–hobby farms owned by core urbanites with core values of free-range and sustainable agriculture.

Buck has been lobbying to no avail for an open season on dairy and beef cattle that escape the farmer's fence; this would lower the methane gas level in the atmosphere, caused by their artificially manipulated diet. As can be expected, his effort has been thwarted by the large domestic animal lobby but has stimulated interest in an ungulate-size Beano® tablet. His efforts to free hogs and the kid's pony for a legal roadkill rodeo are also not bearing fruit.

DAILY SPECIALS

There is no reason why your daily special can't be a chicken, domesticated duck, or goose, and hobby farms located far from the main road are the best places to shop. Hobby farm owners are less likely to own a shotgun, and if they do, most are uncertain which end goes boom. Stealth is a virtue in these shopping runs. Your odds of being spotted increase substantially if you run partway up the drive to purchase a fat organic bird, but less so if you run "dark," without headlights, shopping at dawn and dusk.

Buck's Quick Tip: Free-range domestic birds often attract wild birds. A ring-necked pheasant can be a welcome bonus.

Insects

These ye may eat: the locust after his kind, and the bald locust after his kind, and the beetle after his kind, and the grasshopper after his kind.

—Leviticus 11:22. Amen to this.

Insect flesh is composed of substances similar to those in larger animals and considered an eco-friendly protein source by many cultures. Entomophagy, or insect eating, is practiced in many parts of our country and Buck encourages an open mind for these mostly vegetarian animals while road shopping. He does draw the line on preparing the dung beetle, unless your mother-in-law is coming for dinner. Youngsters love bugs and this culinary exercise can also double as a biology lesson.

The most likely candidates for a roadside buffet are water beetles, grasshoppers, crickets, worms, and caterpillars.

Sweet and Crunchy Insects

1 handful insects

½ cup extra-virgin olive oil

¼ cup honey

Wash and clean the insects, and pat dry. In a skillet, heat the oil over medium-high heat and fry the insects until crispy. Dip in honey and serve. Serves two.

Buck's Quick Tip: For anyone who has traveled to northern Minnesota for a family reunion, there is satisfaction in taking a bite out of the insect kingdom that feasted on you and yours.

Vegetables

When it comes to vegetable shopping, Buck didn't just fall off the turnip truck. He has fallen off the wagon a number of times and when this happens, Good Samaritans help him find his way to a less familiar part of the food pyramid.

Farmers' crops are subject to fluctuations in supply and demand, and underwritten by taxpayer subsidies (from you and me). A farmer's commercial crops are ripe for the pickings, so to speak. Shop as far away from the farmhouse as you can and never take more than you can use unless you are really hungry. If you see a tractor heading your way, skedaddle.

Buck's Quick Tip: The normal range of a 12-gauge shotgun is less than 75 yards.

The vegetable section of Mother Nature's supermarket is just down the road a ways, not far from the meat counter. Much like at your favorite greengrocer, there are distinct shopping sections:

CORN

No vegetable says "summer" more than fresh corn on the cob. Although corn snots may lobby for their favorites—sweet versus supersweet, yellow versus white versus multicolor—few vegetables so nicely complement a meal-on-the-go. And the fresher, the better, as the sugar in corn starts turning to starch as soon as it's picked. Roasted over an open fire, a fresh ear of corn is a colorful accompaniment for pork and upland bird entrées, and a good source of vitamin A.

Corn on the Rob 'er Cob

2 freshly picked ears per person, unhusked

On a skewer of your fashion, hold over an open fire, turning occasionally for 7 to 8 minutes, until the husk is charred. To serve, brush the grilled corn with garlic-salt-infused butter and sprinkle with ground black pepper, or brush with mayonnaise and sprinkle with cayenne. You can also strip kernels off the cob for use in tacos.

APPLES

The satisfaction of stopping by an apple orchard in eastern Washington and grabbing a fresh Delicious apple off the tree cannot be missed. If you need a larger quantity of apples, tie a rope to the tree trunk and shake it hard a couple of times, using the lower gears of your truck transmission. Remember, deer like them apples, too.

TUBERS

The most easily acquired root vegetable is the ordinary potato, gathered catch-as-catch-can behind harvest trucks in eastern Washington and Oregon and Idaho. The most prized "catches" are the potatoes served under Golden Arches and in other fast-food kingdoms.

Roasted Road Russets

2 pounds rescued potatoes, cut into wedges

¼ cup chopped white onion

**¼ cup seeded and chopped red or
yellow bell pepper**

A full twist of the black pepper mill

A pinch of sea salt

1 teaspoon fresh rosemary, chopped

3 tablespoons extra-virgin olive oil

Heat the oven to 425°F. In a mixing bowl, combine all the ingredients. Spread the potato mixture on a greased or nonstick pan and bake for 30 minutes, stirring and turning until the potatoes are tender and golden brown. Serves four.

GREENS

Serious organic shoppers opt for greens found in natural settings. "Oh, fiddle-faddle," you say? Well, some people like fiddlehead ferns, and dandelion leaves, chickweed, and other garden weeds, and smoke their share of homegrown weed, too. No disrespect intended, but these shoppers are the human equivalent of the common goat, yet can't compete with forest animals when it comes to eating small saplings because humans cannot pass bark without the risk of rectal scarring.

Buck's Bonus Tip: If you are indeed what you eat, avoid fruits, nuts, and vegetables. This tip does not apply to animal meat unless you want to clear a fence like a whitetail buck.

Eating Dirt

One possible objection to shopping roadside is the thought of eating dirty food. Although recipes assume the shopper will thoroughly wash the free groceries before preparing the meal, a small defense of eating dirt is in order.

Geophagy, the habit of eating dirt (or clay or mud), has worldwide, centuries-old cultural roots, particularly among women who are pregnant and really, really hungry. Although little research has been done on the value of eating plain old dirt or its liquid form, mud, anecdotal evidence of the health benefits of adding a little clay to the diet is clear—the binding effect of clay is thought to help absorb plant toxins. The minerals in some clay, such as calcium, copper, iron, and magnesium, are essential to the human diet, especially during stress periods such as pregnancy and constipation. Dirt eaters have their favorites—especially in the South, where white clay, a source of kaolin, an antacid found in drugstore medicines for stomach upsets, is found. Don't worry about baking your fresh meats in clay. This information may help overcome any objections of your pregnant spouse on the value of your road-roasted possum. You're welcome, big guy.

Except for the anal-retentive raccoon, healthy wild animals do not wash the dirt from their food, either, and it's unlikely they would even if they had a sink handy.

Editor's Note: The experience of eating clay and out of a clay pot appeals to the sixth sense and, for the latter, Paula Wolfert's publisher. The road from a bird baked in clay to a homemade backyard clay oven is a short one.

How to Shop, Essential Gear, Be a Responsible (Green) Roadside Shopper

How to Shop

CASH FOR THUMPERS

As all supermarket shoppers know, carts are necessary to assemble and transport the groceries to the spawn at home. That can't be truer than with your road cart. Your choices of motorized shopping cart are many: old and new, car and truck, SUV and van. The choice in each category increases every year, especially when it comes to features.

The bumper is the preferred feature on a personal shopping cart. The problem is that ordinary bumpers are not designed to be collection devices. Bumpers are designed only to protect key features of the vehicle under very low speed conditions "equivalent to a 5-mile-per-hour crash into a parked vehicle of the same weight," according to the National Highway Traffic Safety Administration. What this official, responsibility-dodging, Detroit-pandering, blah-blah means is you are on your own, Pilgrim, when the "no damage limit" is applied to a stationary object the size and weight of a mature bull elk. Older American-built cars had steel bumpers that afforded the illusion of some cab safety, but they were removed when automakers noted the lack of heavy steel bumpers on county fair bumper cars. This created the automobile repair industry.

Gasoline/electric-powered shopping cart designers now focus on the ultra-urban car with the single goal of creating a car that is easy to park, and have a deer join you as a passenger on an uncontrolled spin in the countryside. Green auto designers haven't been successful in creating a wind-powered vehicle. Seems the front-mounted propellers only create lift, and cause air turbulence for your lane if mounted instead in the rear.

Good cost-saving advice is to make do with what you have. If you are like everybody else and can't get bank financing for a new shopping cart, strap on the 18- to 22-inch grill from your kettledrum barbecue for a little "grill-on-grille" action—easy to remove, ready to heat.

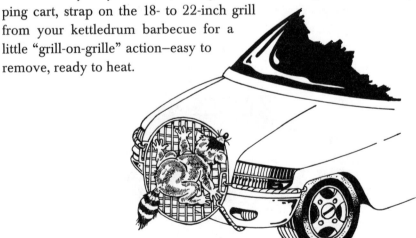

Buck's favorite cart is an old Toyota Land Cruiser, heavier and handier than a Ford 150 (a strong contender), with a steel bumper, light guards, stick shift with a very strong low gear, a rear bumper hook to drag a large purchase out of sight, and an interior cab that can carry a small herd of purchases. Buck's auto design team has been working, however, on a new or retrofit design to move purchases from market to Mom with no fuss, no muss. Readers who paid full price for this book are welcome to cut out this design and take it to their local chop shop for personal use.

Buck's Quick Tip: Actively used shopping carts can be impounded for evidence of wrongful behavior by the game warden. Recommendation: Register this vehicle in your mother's or brother-in-law's name.

THE NEW CAR ADVANTAGE

The single advantage of a new shopping cart is the technology that enables the shopper to see a full meal deal through fog, rain, and darkness. This technology eliminates the element of surprise in less-than-optimal shopping conditions, and is only found in the more expensive models. The need is not new, as Germans have tried to run over the French for years.

Pretechnology, the view out the windshield looked much like this:

In the new, pricey models, the view looks like this:

Detroit automakers have created emergency systems with varying service levels in select models, should your shopping cart's air bag deploy and/or tip over. In an emergency, rescue and medical personnel are called immediately to the scene of the accident. The biggest disadvantage (other than cost) to this system is that emergency personnel have families to feed too, and by alerting strangers that road shopping has been successful, they arrive with a healthy appetite. There are tales of collusion between sheriff deputies and medics who keep whitetail deer on oxygen in the ambulance until surgeons can remove the tastiest cuts for the physicians' cafeteria. The largest advantage of such systems is you can program preferred traffic routes through the areas large tasty animals are likely to frequent at different times of the day.

SHOPPING CART CARE

- Keep the tires fully inflated and check for slow leaks caused by bone chips and beaks.

- Check the fluids on a regular basis, especially coolant. Radiators are often punctured by large animal headgear.

- Change the air filter frequently if shopping off-road in dusty areas. Filters full of feathers also result in less-than-peak cart performance.

- Check the windshield wipers for damage. Replace the wipers and side mirrors if missing from an interaction.

- Inspect the battery cables and posts for looseness. The battery must be tightly secured for the active shopper.

- Replace the headlights, turn signals, and windshield at your earliest convenience, to avoid attention from hungry game wardens.

- The brakes often need attention, especially in areas where endangered species live.

- Check the shocks and suspension equipment on a regular basis to make sure they are able and stable to handle off-road shopping.

- Keep the engine in tune so your cart is first to arrive in a large animal migration and first to depart when the heat is on.

- For best shopping results, practice driving down ditches and through large culverts, game tunnels, and hobby farmer front yards.

Essential Gear

APPAREL

An apron two sizes larger than normal is necessary for wraparound comfort and cover. Have a red apron for roadwork, a blue apron for on-air work, and a white apron for entertaining out-of-town guests. Also wear a toque or top hat with a band stuffed with tail feathers in full display. Holiday dress should match the occasion—a Thanksgiving roadside chef should look like a pilgrim, updated as needed. Buckle galoshes are an acceptable substitute for high-buckle shoes.

OIL (COOKING)

Buck's favorite cooking oil is Crisco® in a can. Buck's cardiologist and other nosy individuals tout the Mediterranean diet for a long life and recommend the exclusive use of extra-virgin olive oil for field and home. As if virginity is a prized virtue in that sated southern region. At home, unsalted butter in huge quantities is recommended. Then add more butter. Infuse it and use it!

SPICES

Salt and pepper are staples in most recipes. Road-salted rib eyes call for gourmet salt. Kosher and/or sea salt, garlic salt, and ground black or multicolored peppercorns in a 6-inch Unicorn grinder are in Buck's culinary toolbox. Brave shoppers always carry bold mustard; anything Dijon works, and mixed with olive oil–based mayonnaise, it is especially good for dried thin meat. Grey Poupon mustard is a great coating for upland birds, especially when the feathers are removed.

Hot enough for you this summer? Eat spicy foods. They raise your

body temperature and make you sweat, and sweating helps you cool down. If you don't want to grind peppers in your food stash, carry a shaker of crushed roasted red peppers and, for upland birds, a jar of spicy peanut sauce. Quick-Fix road meats never need meat tenderizers.

TOOLS

A garlic press (an OXO® steel garlic press will do), a set of bird shears, a set of CUTCO® barbecue tools, a grill basket, and a heavy oven mitt are important, along with a meat thermometer, knives, cast-iron pan, and Dutch oven. Also grab any syringe from a vet supply house, for injection cooking. In the field, have a long-handled shovel to bury the remains, a rake to make the ground nice and level, and wildflower seeds to leave the scene of your interaction a better place than you found it.

MISCELLANEOUS

Keep a supply of wood chips—hickory, apple, and mesquite—to drop on your field fire and charcoal grill at home. Paraffin-soaked cotton balls or clothes dryer lint lit with a windproof lighter are foolproof fire starters. Life in the fast-food lane shouldn't be complicated. As mentioned earlier, all you need is a sharpened stick, a book of matches from Buck's Valhalla Lounge, and a song in your heart.

Be a Responsible (Green) Roadside Shopper

Keep your tires at the optimum pressure. Underinflation will increase wear, as well as reduce fuel economy by several percentage points and thus your ability to shop smartly.

If you aren't planning to shop for a large animal, remove the rooftop carrier to substantially improve your fuel economy. Empty your trunk.

If you have to drive any distance to reach the busy wild game supermarkets, use cruise control and overdrive to save gas. If you are a member of an automobile club, have the staff map out the shortest distance for you or simply use a GPS unit.

Whenever possible, combine normal family activities such as taking the kids to school and road shopping on the way home. Carpool with friends and work associates of like mind. Make sure you decide in advance how a large purchase will be shared, and divide the off-road responsibilities.

How to Tell When an Animal Has Given Up the Ghost

A sure sign that your meal is ready for speedy handling is the condition of its eyes. If the eyes are wide open and crossed:

Your efforts were negligible.

When the eyes are wide open, focused, and angry:

Your best course of action is to hurry home and hide in the closet.

If the eyes are cloudy:

**The animal has passed on to the Magic Kingdom
or has glaucoma and is too tough to eat.**

An indication of table-ready steaks:

If you are still not sure if that small car–size animal sleeping on the shoulder has gone to Disneyland, there are several other methods to determine when to wrap your purchase.

1. Poke it with a sharp stick.

2. Poke it again.

3. Pull its tail.

4. For a bull, kick it in the nut-sack.

5. For a bull, have your Jack Russell terrier bite it in the nut-sack.

6. For a cow or doe, have your Jack Russell terrier mount it from the rear.

That should do it. If you are taking the purchase whole, do not carry it in the passenger compartment unless the children need a playmate in the backseat.

Methods of Preparation

BAKING

Many familiar recipes call for baking wild game at 350°F for 3 hours, or 3°F for 350 hours. Buck forgets which one is preferred. Disregard these non-quick-fix recipes. If you have a large-size chunk of meat, cut it into minute steaks.

BARBECUE VERSUS GRILLING

Roadkill cooking is largely determined by the preferred time and place. If time is short and the place is near, grilling—the application of direct heat to your meat—is a shortcut to meals-on-the-go. True barbecue requires slow-roasting meat with indirect heat and smoke over longer periods of time.

Grilling in the field: There is no reason to carry a fancy, large grill while shopping for the family, but if you have room in the pickup bed, many street people insist the best grill is the one provided by the other kind of supermarket. The first use of this shopping cart will burn off any corporate logos.

At home: The choices are between a gas grill (propane or natural gas) and a charcoal grill. Enough has been written about the pros and the cons of both, but note that most pros and a few cons prefer the Weber® charcoal grill to cook for themselves and family.

Don't be in such a hurry to empty your open ash catcher. Small birds enjoy dusting in the cool ash.

HOW HOT IS THE GRILL, OR WHEN DO WE EAT?

If you can keep your hand 5 inches over the source of heat for:

Less than 1 second–about right; if you can't stand the heat, get out of Buck's dream kitchen (see page 119)

1 to 2 seconds–hot

3 to 4 seconds–medium-hot

5 to 6 seconds–low; get out the s'mores

> **Buck's Quick Tip:** For vegetarians, the above test will not work while wearing gardening gloves.

BOILING

For this preparation, you only need a pot, water, and heat. Boiling road meat can, however, make it tough, and the water cannot be used for drinking without filtering. Some boil tough cuts over low heat for a long period of time. Disregard this non-Quick-Fix preparation, too.

FRYING

Wild game meat belongs in a hot cast-iron skillet, in unsalted butter. A cast-iron skillet sheds the minerals that build strong bones. The skillet's edges hold wild mushrooms and wild onions, and you can pan-fry Highway Smashed Browns (page 100) in the drippings. The results will make you slap her mama's mama.

INJECTION

Are you on pins and needles that your recipe won't be perfect, regardless of method of preparation? Consider injection cooking. Upland birds can be improved by injecting your choice of taste enhancers, not the gray water, used motor oil, and assorted factory worker bodily fluids used by domestic processors. Enhancers range from softened, salted butter (use Land O'Lakes® butter–the pretty Indian princess on the box will appreciate it), Italian salad dressing, a good crab boil, and actually any other liquid flavor that can pass through a large hypodermic needle or kit injector.

ROASTING

Who hasn't hummed "Chestnuts Roasting on an Open Fire," regardless of the season? The preferred Quick-Fix preparation requires only a stick and an open fire. How good does that get? For the almost quick-fix preparation, you need only a grill, an open fire, and a set of tongs or a multitool.

How to Tell
When Your Meal Is Ready

The Touch Test

Experienced hands use their paws to judge the doneness of a road purchase. With the index finger of your dominant hand, touch the base of your thumb on the other hand. That is the softness of rare steak. Now touch the thumb with the middle finger on that hand and then touch the base of the thumb with your dominant finger, and you are moving toward a medium-rare steak. The ring finger touch is medium-well and when you touch the connection between your thumb and pinkie, your thumb will feel like a steak your blue healer wouldn't eat without a beer to wash it down.

This test works best when the cook has all his or her digits and not wearing an oven mitt, frying testicles, or signing to a deaf person.

Using a Meat Thermometer

Meat thermometers take the guesswork out of road cooking by accurately measuring the internal temperature and telling you when it's safe to eat. An instant-read stainless-steel thermometer is the best.

WHERE TO INSERT A MEAT THERMOMETER

Upland Birds and Waterfowl: Insert the thermometer into the inner thigh near the breast but not touching any bones.

Small and Big Game: Insert the thermometer in the thickest part of the meat, away from bones and any live explosives.

WHEN TO INSERT A MEAT THERMOMETER

When you are unsure. How? Insert at least 2 inches into the meat and wait for a reading to appear in 10 to 15 seconds.

MINIMUM INTERNAL COOKING TEMPERATURES (ROAD FRESH)

Red meat (whole)	145°F (medium-rare)
White meat (whole)	145°F (medium-rare)
Ground round	160°F
Upland birds (whole)	175°F

Leftovers, or
Remains of the Day

There is no reason to be greedy when the free, open-air supermarket is so large. In the field, leave something other than the hide, head, and feet for the rest of the meat-eating animal kingdom. They have nutritional needs as well. You'll promote the circle of life, and give your neighbor's barking dog fun stuff to roll in.

Buck's Quick Tips: The most private parts of an animal are stored in a nice bag inside. Do what you can to remove that bag intact for a clean deposit on your brother-in-law's doorstep.

Generous shoppers also leave innards behind so little bitty and senior critters can enjoy a free meal. This gesture promotes the selfless vision of the Meals Under Wheels Foundation®.

Gourmands cherry-pick the gift-bag selection for tasty treats rarely found in your ordinary supermarket. Recipes for exotic meats, from nose to toes and lips to hips, are found on page 129.

Quick-Fix Recipes Anyone Can Cook

hree squares a day, at home, at work, on the go. Fast and fresh! Delicious (simple, yummy) meals in 30 minutes or less for breakfast, brunch, lunch, dinner, and in-between snacks.

Deep-Ditch Pizza

Freeway Frittata

Croaked Frogs' Legs

Grand Slam Burger

Grand Slam Sliders

The Grateful Dead

Shish Kaboom Kebabs

Street Meatballs

Wrecktangle MeataBall

Baby Cracked Ribs

Pavement Panini

Tar-tare

Deep-Ditch Pizza

Kids love pizza, and parents do, too, because making pizza is easy and fun. Pizza counters estimate that every American man, woman, and child consumes an average of forty-six pizza slices a year, and all on the same day in Little Italy. All you need for Deep-Ditch Pizza is pizza dough that can be prepared on a grill over an open fire, plus fresh toppings. The topping ingredients purchased in and on the way into a deep ditch couldn't be fresher. Throw a pizza party.

1 (10-ounce) package pizza dough

2 tablespoons extra-virgin olive oil

TOPPINGS:

Assorted road-cured meats

¼ cup prepared tomato sauce

¼ cup wild onions, sliced

¼ cup blue cheese, crumbled

¼ cup mozzarella cheese, sliced

**¼ cup seeded and chopped chile peppers,
any color and heat**

¼ cup sliced forest mushrooms

¼ cup fresh basil or fresh rosemary, chopped

Prepare the dough according to the package directions and roll out on waxed paper. With tongs, flip dough side down onto a medium-hot grill. Peel off the paper and cook until grill marks appear. Lift off the grill, brush with oil, and load with toppings (except greens) on the grill-mark side. Return the pizza to the grill, naked dough side down, and cover. Cook for 5 minutes, or until the cheese is melted. Serves four hungry party animals.

Buck's Quick Tip: When building your fire, add aromatic wood chips for that special smoky flavor.

Freeway Frittata

Freeway frittatas combine the better of two possible worlds—eggs borrowed from the hobby farmer's henhouse and fresh meat gathered from your grille. A frittata is usually prepared in a skillet, but there is no reason you can't create a splendid omelet on a hot, flat surface under the hood.

4 chicken, 6 pheasant, or 12 robin eggs

⅓ teaspoon ground black pepper

A pinch of salt

1 teaspoon unsalted butter

⅓ cup chopped road meat

⅓ cup chopped road vegetables

In a mixing bowl, combine the eggs, pepper, and salt. Heat the butter in a pan over an available medium-heat source. Add the meat and vegetables and sauté for 2 minutes. Pour the egg mixture over the meat and vegetables and gently stir. Cook for 5 minutes, or until the egg mixture starts to set up, then carefully fold and flip. Cover and heat for another 5 minutes, until the frittata is lightly browned. Remove from the pan and serve immediately. Serves two.

If you haven't tried a Freeway Frittata, the terrorists have won.

—Asphalt Annie, Homeland Security Mobile Unit

Buck's Quick Tip: Substitute ⅓ cup of wild mushrooms for common road vegetables. The effects of psychedelic mushrooms depend on quantity and personal metabolism.

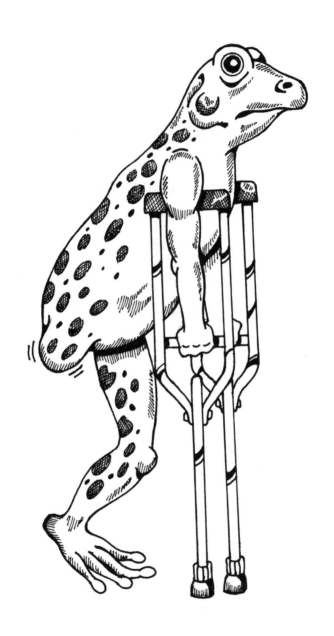

Croaked Frogs' Legs

On dark, rainy nights, American bullfrogs come out of the swamps to audition for beer commercials and provide road shoppers with an excellent opportunity to gather a bucket of legs akimbo. Often growing as big as 8 inches long and weighing up to 3 pounds, a large bullfrog is loath to give up its means of locomotion, so a head shot is recommended.

**4 frog legs (back only),
removed at the hip and skinned**

3 tablespoons unsalted butter

1 cup seasoned all-purpose flour

2 eggs, beaten

1 cup cracker meal

Soak the legs in salted water for 2 hours and pat dry. In a skillet, melt the butter over medium-high heat. Roll the legs in the flour and fry until golden brown. Serves one.

VARIATIONS: Dip the legs into 2 beaten eggs and roll in 1 cup of cracker meal. Replace the butter with 1 cup of extra-virgin olive oil and fry until golden brown.

Roll the legs in flour as above and fry in extra-virgin olive oil with 2 crushed garlic cloves until golden brown.

- -

Buck's Quick Tips: Bullfrogs got their name from their deep call (jug-o-rum) that to some sounds like a bull having its testicles removed (see Testicle Festival, page 87). A bullfrog's call can be heard for over a quarter of a mile, more than that if it's missing a leg or two.

It takes two to four years for a tadpole to grow a nice set of gams. It takes at least fifteen years for a Hollywood starlet, less than that for a harlot.

A Bullfrog cocktail is made of equal portions rum, gin, tequila, and blue Curaçao poured over ice in a highball glass, topped by a can of Red Bull. Several of these will make you croak.

- -

Grand Slam Burger

The hamburger originated in the German town of Hamburg. Imagine the confusion of NASCAR and Chicago Cubs fans if the hamburger had been first served in Frankfurt.

Grand Slam Burgers are filled with an all-meat patty, game or red meat mixed with the other white meat. Elk, moose, and deer are the most commonly used road meats and often mixed with more fatty meats, such as pork, for flavor and moisture. The recommended percentage of fat is 25 percent.

2 pounds red ground round

1 pound ground pork

6 soft hamburger buns (alternatives: poppy-seed or onion bagels, or glazed doughnuts)

TOPPINGS:

Bacon slices

Tomato slices

Chili

Barbecue sauce

Peanut butter

Caramelized or raw onions

Cheese

Condiments

In a mixing bowl, combine the ground round and pork. Form into patties about 1 inch thick, packing the burger meat loosely. Grill over a hot fire or in a preheated skillet over medium heat for 3 minutes per side. Don't squash with your spatula. Toast the buns over the fire as well and pile on your favorite toppings when done. Serves six.

Buck's Quick Tips: Respect your shopping area by choosing local cheeses: cheese curds in Wisconsin; Tillamook sharp cheddar in Oregon; and pressurized-can cheese in Alabama, Mississippi, and Arkansas. Look for the presidential seal on the commemorative cheese can at the William Jefferson Clinton Library gift shop in Little Rock.

When adding cheese, leave the burger on the heat until the cheese is completely melted. For extra flavor, top with crushed jalapeño-flavored Tim's Potato Chips or Doritos® Diablo Flavored Tortilla Chips.

Grand Slam Sliders

Looking for small bites? Look no further. Sliders are today's answer to the small plate question. Buck's first taste of sliders was the commercially made variety. A special road game on the Twin City beltline was to grab a bag of White Castle sliders and pitch them from a top-down Austin Healy 106 to friends racing along the freeway. A waste of a steamed bun wrapped around a square meat patty covered with smashed onions? Sure, but it was less dangerous than text messaging, whatever that is.

Divide 1 pound of ground round into 8 equal portions and fix like the regular burger above. Serve in 2 miniature potato flour buns.

Playing Possum

Possums seem like such fun animals. They like to play games with the roadside shopper. When they seem threatened, the funny marsupials play dead like children asked to clean up their room. However, possums know only one game. They don't know how to play hide-and-seek or jump rope or any of the recent Wii games. And the latter should be easy with their opposable thumbs. That inability is fatal when compared to other more childlike, athletic animals. When male "Jack" and female "Jill" possums take a human's road up the hill, their karma turns bad. Mammal mystics believe that road possums return as highway department–installed speed bumps.

Possum meat has long enjoyed a table tradition, especially for people who can't spell opossum, and tastes as you'd expect. Possums are omnivores with a preference for roadkill, and this makes them competitors for your vittles. Their final deserts are more than just.

Before cooking, make sure the possum isn't playing possum by lying next to it and having a pal watch if the eye opens on the other side of the head. If not, pick up the possum by the tail and swing it really fast around your head. If you don't hear the possum version of "Whee!" assume it's time to find 'taters to go with your road purchase.

The Grateful Dead

**1 possum the size of a large house cat,
but better tasting**

Salt and ground black pepper

1 cup prepared dressing

Preheat the oven to 350°F. Scald the carcass and scrape off the body hair. Dress and wash the animal completely. For parties, leave the head and tail intact. Place the possum in a deep pan on its back and arrange its paws so the animal looks peaceful, like Uncle Bob at the funeral home. Don't forget to put a small bouquet of parsley in its paws before serving. Fill the pan with enough water to cover the possum to its navel, wherever the navel is. Bake for 1 hour, then salt and pepper the cavity and stuff with the dressing. Reposition the possum, belly up, in its final roasting place, with yams or sweet potatoes as a crown, and bake until golden brown. Serves as many as you'd think.

Shish Kaboom Kebabs
(Colloquial: Shish Boom-Bah Kebabs)

Shish kebabs are the perfect on-the-go meal. They can be made in advance of your road-shopping ka-boom and accommodate every taste and appetite with different combinations of meats, fruits, and vegetables. Kids in particular love meat on a stick.

Red and white fresh game meat (pork and upland birds); sirloin tip if eating alone

Canned chunk-style pineapple

Fresh coconut

Bell peppers (green, red, yellow, orange)

Cherry tomatoes

Apples

Canned small potatoes

Zucchini

Whole large mushrooms

Eggplant

Jalapeño peppers

Sweet onions

Sweet potato

Squash

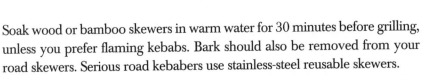

Soak wood or bamboo skewers in warm water for 30 minutes before grilling, unless you prefer flaming kebabs. Bark should also be removed from your road skewers. Serious road kebabers use stainless-steel reusable skewers.

Cut all the ingredients into bite-size pieces; 1 inch for most, 4 inches for her mother. Parboil all the vegetables and fruits except the potatoes and tomatoes. Disregard the parboiling step if you like vegetables with snap. Thread onto the skewers, taking great care to give plenty of space between

the pieces; ½ inch should do. For a colorful presentation, alternate the road meat with fruits and vegetables. Those who suffer from sodium deficiency can wrap the meat bits in thick-cut bacon strips. Brush the vegetables with olive oil; sprinkle with your favorite spices or sauces. Some recommendations: chile pepper and cumin for lamb, soy sauce for upland birds.

Grill the kebabs over medium-high heat for the meat to reach medium-rare, 10 to 12 minutes, rotating several times. Bread chunks (use crusted Italian bread cut into small cubes and brushed with olive oil or butter with garlic salt) threaded onto additional skewers and browned over the same fire are a delightful accompaniment. Serve one or two skewers per person.

Buck's Quick Tips: If you have already purchased your road meat, consider using a marinade to add flavor. Place the meat chunks in a marinade of your favorite salad dressing or any combination of soy sauce, red wine, brown sugar, garlic, extra-virgin olive oil infused with rosemary, and marjoram (lamb) or curry (upland birds) in a heavy plastic bag for several hours or overnight in a refrigerator.

The term *shish kebab* originated in Turkey and means "skewered roasted meat." Then, as now, kebabs fit the nomad lifestyle, although with the introduction of studded tires, there is no longer a need to tenderize trail meat under the saddle.

Buck's favorite kebab is lamb, which is difficult to procure unless Mary had a little lamb with fleece as white as snow wandering down the centerline of the road from the hobby farm. Marinate in salsa verde and Middle Eastern spices, and serve with plain or flavored yogurt. Or frozen yogurt.

Editor's Note: Kebab, Kabob, Kabeb, Billy Joe Bob . . . will someone out there in culinary language land settle on one spelling?

Street Meatballs

⅓ **pound red ground round**

⅓ **pound ground wild boar**

⅓ **pound ground whitetail fawn
or robin breasts**

1 clove garlic, minced

1 teaspoon kosher salt

⅓ **teaspoon ground black pepper**

2 tablespoons extra-virgin olive oil

In a mixing bowl, combine all the ingredients except the olive oil. Roll the mixture into 1-inch balls. Heat the olive oil in a nonstick pan over moderate heat and add the meatballs. Turning occasionally, cook for 7 to 8 minutes, until browned. Serves five persons with six meatballs each, six persons with five meatballs each, two persons with fifteen meatballs each, or fifteen persons with two balls, nut-sack not included.

VARIATIONS: For Great Balls of Fire, add 2 tablespoons of Buck's Go-to-Hell-in-a-Handbasket Sauce before combining the ingredients.

For Great Balls of China, add 2 tablespoons of MSG before combining the ingredients and wrap each cooked meatball in a piece of Bibb lettuce. See Testicle Festival (page 87) for other variations.

Wrecktangle MeataBall

1 recipe Meatballs

Preheat the oven to 350°F. Instead of forming into balls, press the mixture into a greased 9 by 5-inch loaf pan. Bake for 30 minutes, let cool, and slice. Serve open faced on artisan bread, with pepper Jack cheese melted on top. Don't let your meat loaf! Serve hot. Serves four.

This Little Piggy Went to Market

The most useful meat animal is the domestic pig. Along with its woodland cousin, it is a regular item on the road-shopping list. Wild pigs found on the roadways are darker, larger, and leaner escapees from commercial farms that have turned feral or are abandoned Vietnamese potbellied pigs who outgrew their welcome. Prepared properly, pork is never a culinary bore for your table guests.

Tout est bon dans un cochun.
(Everything on a pig is useful.)

Baby Cracked Ribs

Don't let the illustration fool you. Baby back ribs aren't taken from baby pigs. If they were, the pig's belly would drag on the ground. Baby back ribs are taken from market-weight hogs, not sows, and are a popular party favor.

2 racks baby back ribs

Salt and ground black pepper

SAUCE:

2 tablespoons Dijon mustard

1 tablespoon honey

2 tablespoons dark brown sugar

1 tablespoon cider vinegar, or to taste

2 cloves garlic, minced

Preheat the oven to 350°F. Remove the tough membrane from the underside of the ribs, and dust both sides with salt and pepper. Place bone side down in a baking dish and cover with foil. Bake for 1 hour, or until the meat starts pulling from the bone. In a mixing bowl, combine the sauce ingredients and brush the ribs. Turn the ribs over and return to the oven for 10 minutes. Reverse the ribs and glaze again. Bake as above and serve. Serves two when the gang is pigging out.

Buck's Quick Tips: Stack the ribs casually on a big platter, leaning against one another or crosshatched like a small campfire.

These ribs are good enough to slap your mama. Add a few tall brews and you'll be brave enough to slap *her* mama. Good luck.

Pavement Panini

The most popular meal for lunch and dinner in America is the sandwich. The breakfast sandwich is not far behind, especially for those who sleep in. The ease and convenience of a sandwich meets our on-the-go culture with a hot variation of the toasted sandwich called panini, *an Americanized, plural version of the Italian* panino, *or small sandwich. Panini are available in supermarkets and at home, where busy parents with a panini grill try to fool their children that their lunch is not just another grilled sandwich.*

For the roadside shopper, pavement panini offer a wide variety of ingredients and interesting bread tread designs. If you are able to bump an egg out of an upland bird, add the ingredient for a breakfast panini.

**2 slices bread for each serving, artisan bread
such as focaccia or ciabetta preferred**

Cheese, sliced thickly

Tomato, sliced

Lettuce, if available

Road meat, sliced thinly

Assemble the ingredients into a sandwich. On a nice warm day, roll over the sandwich just once before serving. On a nice cold day, roll over the sandwich and let warm tires (from skidding) finish combining the ingredients. On a blistering cold day, grill the sandwich once you've marked it with your tire tread.

Preferred Panini Tires

All-Weather/Season Tires: The most common, least expensive tires for roadside shoppers, designed for soft comfort in dry and rainy conditions alike. The simplest of tire designs.

Performance Tires: High-performance tires are perfect for road shoppers living in a highly competitive shopping environment and/or for fast getaways.

Competition Tires: Built specifically for racing shopping carts, these groove-free tires will not leave the desired pattern on your finished panini.

Snow Tires: Manufacturers recommend selecting a narrow winter tire for easier passage in heavy snow. A lower pressure reading cushions the purchase and expands the wider-spaced tread design.

Studded Tires: Useful for eliminating a step in preparation by tenderizing your fresh purchase, not to mention giving you more control of your shopping cart.

Chains: When combined with a good winch, these allow the winter shopper a wider selection of wild game meat markets and greater off-road reach.

Truck Tires: Provide good traction for on- and off-road use, but the serious shopper prefers all-terrain tires.

Tar-Tare

The quickest and freshest road snack is ground round or round ground. Tartare, raw minced steak, has its origins with the Tatars (not the Mongol family that invented tartar sauce—the other family, the ones on the spotted ponies to the left of the steppes in the reunion picture). The Tatars shredded their low-quality, tough meat to make it easier to chew and digest, when they didn't have studded Uniroyals® to help.

1 pound fresh backstrap, red game meat, or steak

4 medium-size white anchovies, chopped

3 teaspoons capers, drained and rinsed

4 teaspoons Dijon mustard

3 large egg yolks

2 tablespoons chopped red onion

5 tablespoons extra-virgin olive oil

Salt and ground black pepper

Chop the meat and refrigerate for at least 2 hours. In a mixing bowl, combine the anchovies, capers, and mustard, and mix well. Add the meat, egg yolks, onions, and oil, mix well, and add salt and pepper to taste. Serve on garlic toast points. Serves four.

VARIATION:

**1 pound fresh backstrap,
red game meat, or steak**

4 egg yolks

4 medium-size white anchovies, chopped finely

4 tablespoons capers, drained and rinsed

1 cup minced white onions

**2 hard-boiled large eggs,
peeled and chopped**

Chop the meat and divide into 4-ounce patties. With a spoon, make a small round indentation in the middle of each patty and place a fresh egg yolk in the hollow. In a mixing bowl, combine the anchovies, capers, onions, and eggs. Place equal portions on chilled plates and serve with toast points. Serves four.

Buck's Quick Tip: Raw and undercooked wild pig meat has a history of carrying trichinosis, a potentially fatal disease if left untreated. Ditto for bear. Raw meat must be absolutely fresh and not from an area where large game animals carry any herd diseases. The safest choice: horse meat. See Kentucky Derby (page 84).

Sunday Family Dinner ("Weekends Are Made for Michelins"): Mom's Home Cooking

Mom's Favorite Roadkill Recipe

A staple in the Midwest for social gatherings, especially potlucks, is the casserole or hot dish. The variety found in church basements and home kitchens is overwhelming and Buck's mom's contribution is one of the first to be eaten up. This recipe is fast and easy to prepare, can accommodate a medley of road groceries, and tastes good, too.

Peasant Pheasant Supreme

2 tablespoons extra-virgin olive oil

1 pheasant, plucked, cleaned, and cut up

1 (2-ounce) package instant onion soup mix

1 (10¾-ounce) can cream of chicken soup

1 (10¾-ounce) can of mushroom soup

2 (10¾-ounce) soup cans of water

1 cup uncooked brown rice

Preheat the oven to 350°F. In a skillet, heat the oil and pan-fry the pheasant. Set aside to cool. In a mixing bowl, combine the remaining ingredients and transfer to a 9 by 13-inch baking pan. Place the pheasant on the rice mixture and bake for 2½ hours. Serves four.

Buck's Quick Tips: Dip an intact pheasant or any upland bird breast in buttermilk and coat with flour or panko. Brown in butter, and using the same browned butter, sauté 4 sliced large white mushrooms. Place the pheasant in a baking pan, cover with the mushrooms and browned butter, and bake at 350°F for 45 to 50 minutes. Serve over cooked rice.

The collection of cans from these recipes can be saved for plinking off a wood fence or in a gravel pit.

Neither Hide nor Hair

10 possums, skinned and boned

1 cup unbleached all-purpose flour

5 tablespoons extra-virgin olive oil

1 quart chicken broth

1 onion, chopped

6 carrots, sliced

3 stalks celery, sliced

1 (12-ounce) package frozen sliced green beans

2 bay leaves

½ teaspoon dried basil

2 teaspoons sea salt

1 teaspoon ground black pepper

Cut the possum into bite-size pieces and roll in the flour. In a Dutch oven, heat the oil and brown the possum. Remove and set aside. Combine the remaining ingredients in the Dutch oven and bring to a boil. Add the possum, cover, and simmer for 45 minutes, or until everything is tender. Remove the bay leaves before serving. If you have late drop-ins, adding small pieces of rabbit can extend this dish, but most people don't like to find hare in their stew.

For the Little Tots

2 pounds ground road meat

2 tablespoons chopped onion

1 (10¾-ounce) can cream of mushroom soup

1 (10¾-ounce) can cream of celery soup

⅓ cup sour cream

1 (10¾-ounce) can green beans

1 (1-pound) bag Tater Tots®

Preheat the oven to 350°F. Combine the road meat and onion, place in a baking pan, and roast until browned. Remove from the oven, drain, and chop. In a mixing bowl, combine the meat, soups, sour cream, and beans. Place one-third of the Tater Tots® in a greased 9 by 13-inch pan. Cover with the meat mixture and top with the remaining Tater Tots. Bake for 30 minutes, or until the Tater Tots® turn golden brown. Serves four to six little tots, or two to four big tots.

Playing with Your Food:
Quick-Fix Recipes for
Kids of All Ages

Children's Favorites

Infants in their highchairs view mealtime as a multiple-activity hour. Finger food is perfect to engage their active minds, so run into Big Bird on *Sesame Street* and serve up a mess of the following:

Upland Bird Fingers

2 pounds pheasant breasts, skinned and boned

⅔ cup all-purpose flour

⅓ teaspoon salt

⅓ teaspoon ground black pepper

1 teaspoon paprika

3 tablespoons butter, melted

Preheat the oven to 425°F. Cut the pheasant crosswise into 1½-inch strips. In a mixing bowl, combine the flour, salt, and spices. Dip the pheasant strips in the butter, then in the flour mixture. Place in a baking pan and bake, uncovered, for 15 minutes. Turn and bake for another 15 minutes. Remove from the oven, let cool, and serve with honey or ketchup dipping sauce. Serves six.

Buck's Quick Tip: For party decorations, boil six pheasant feet in water for 20 minutes, drain, and let cool. The fingers can also be accompanied with pheasant leg bones: Tie knots in the ends of refrigerated bread sticks, brush with butter, and bake according to the package directions. Serve dusted with chili powder for color.

Hungry children can be counted on to present behavioral issues in school, especially for those with parents who put really dumb stuff like fruit in their lunch boxes. Give your kid a leg up on their peer group (and biology class) by packing an animal kingdom not found on the Disney Channel. The class bullies will give your spawn wide berth if they bring along a selection of road-shopping treats.

SCHOOL ZONE

Perky Jerky

Jerky is the perfect snack for the got-to-go-in-a-hurry society. Jerky is light to carry, ready to eat, full of protein, and has a long shelf life. Road jerky is most often found in warm climates and/or in the heat of the summer. For most shoppers, the sun-aged meat patty that stopped being "perky" a while ago is too much an acquired taste. Buck's famous Perky Jerky is in the shape of the animals found most often in your travels and can be a fun food project for the entire family.

5 pounds fresh red road meat

3 tablespoons soy sauce

3 tablespoons red wine

3 teaspoons sea salt

7 tablespoons sugar

½ teaspoon Chinese five-spice powder

Cut the meat into 6-inch-wide strips. Use this template to trim the strips into the shape of a road animal.

In a mixing bowl, combine the remaining ingredients. Place the animal shapes in the marinade and refrigerate for 24 hours. Preheat the oven to 350°F, drain the animal shapes, and place on a baking sheet. Bake for 15 minutes, turning once, or until the critters turn golden brown. Cool and put in the lunch box for the kids in the morning before the bus arrives. Serves the entire fourth-grade class. The teacher may use her hall pass.

Special Entertaining Occasions

Entertaining with Roadkill

With the time and energy dedicated to acquire a fine meal for those at home and special gatherings, you should spend an equal amount in the presentation and serving of your bumper crop.

One of the most popular themed table decorations in Buck's Lodge is called the Open Road.

Serving Trays

Clockwise from upper left: the modern spoke hubcap, standard import hubcap, spinner hubcap, brushed aluminum moon hubcap, wagon wheel hubcap.

The Open Road table consists of a medium gray tablecloth cut to fit a round or rectangular table, with a bright yellow ribbon running down the middle for the centerline. The creative decorator snips the yellow ribbon to denote passing zones and includes narrow white ribbons for marking the edge of the road. The remainder of the decoration provides great fun for the entire family, especially the wee ones: Little Junior's collection of Hot Wheels can be used as shopping carts veering in all directions, with a few off the road on the shoulder, and Sis can supply her miniature animals, such as My Little Pony®. Trees and other natural features from Dad's train set and Mom's Christmas settings complement the entire shopping area. Let your imagination run free. For example, add artificial snow to show how hard it is to stop for a deer in the road. Let the guests choose their own vehicles. Buck guarantees that your Open Road dinner party will become legendary.

As the road-shopping enthusiast might suspect, the most popular serving pieces at Buck's bumper banquets are hubcaps. The variety of shapes and sizes available will excite the guests and tweak fine memories of their first and/or favorite cars. Of course, the modern spoke hubcap holds the small portions or appetizers. Standard import hubcaps are used for the second or main course, and the spinner hubcap from the 1950s fits right into a retro party theme. Buck's favorite serving platter is a brushed aluminum moon hubcap that, combined with removable whitewalls, makes the most elusive girls take a second look at your tricked-out cart. The wagon wheel hubcap appeals to old-timers, especially with fresh road jerky draped over the spokes.

The range of party favors is limited only by the shopper's imagination. A solid relationship with a taxidermist is a boon to those who have the budget to really dress out a party room. Feathers, hides, and assorted animal body parts in the hands of a professional can produce a dining diorama of museum quality.

All-Purpose Entertaining

The Fondue Party

In this blowback to the 1960s, boomers and their boom-box spawn match Quick-Fix cooking with today's eating attributes—the small bites. Given the variety of heat sources from electric to the old-fashioned and often hard to find canned heat such as Sterno®, fondue pots are the perfect Quick-Fix portable at home and on the road.

2 pounds road meat, skinned and cleaned

6 cups peanut or extra-virgin olive oil

1 cup each of favorite dips: brown mustard, soy sauce, teriyaki sauce, creamy horseradish, ketchup, salad dressing

Cut the meat into squares as large as you can swallow: ½ inch for women, 1 inch for men, 4 inches for her mother. Fill a fondue or cast-iron pot with oil to the halfway mark (use chicken broth to cook upland bird pieces) and place on a burner. Heat the oil to almost boiling at 325° to 350°F, when the oil will be moving slightly. Stick a piece of meat into the oil and cook until it reaches your preferred doneness: upland game bird, 1 minute; red meat, 2 to 3 minutes. When the other diners aren't looking, spear theirs. Dip in the sauces and enjoy. Serves four.

Buck's Quick Tip: For a fondue that will make your cardiologist have spasms, use clarified butter in place of the oil. Melt a pound of butter slowly in a pan over low heat and then let stand for 5 minutes. Skim the crud off the top and pour the clear butter into a mason jar (leaving the solid crud on the pan bottom) for later use. This will cook hotter than regular butter.

Author's Note: The fondue party (left) is one that Buck and Sourdough threw in the late 1970s to celebrate the ability to get up in the morning. Sourdough was rarely seen in public due to restraint issues with one of his earlier wives, and everyone agrees he deserved solitary confinement. His new friend from the party left a budding career as a lap dancer in Montreal to help hold his alpine horn on Mount Vernonia.

Kentucky Derby

The first of the three major horse races of the year is a good time to kick off a race of your own. Create a similar environment for this special equine shopping event: white linen suits and toppers for the gentlemen, a pretty yellow dress and floppy hat for that filly on the gent's arm, a thermos filled with mint juleps, a racing form of your equine purchase life list, and a full tank of gas in your shiny new SUV. This makes for a pleasant Sunday drive through suburban horse acres.

Giddyup Eat-It-Up Steak

8 tablespoons (1 stick) unsalted butter

**2 (16-ounce) round steaks
(3-year-old Thoroughbred preferred–look any gift
horse in the mouth and tell its age by tooth wear)**

Salt and ground black pepper

Preheat a cast-iron skillet over medium-high heat. Melt the butter, place the steaks in the pan, and turn after 3 minutes. Cook the other side for 3 minutes. Remove the steaks from the pan, let rest for 3 to 5 minutes (this allows the juices inside to settle down), and season lightly with salt and pepper. Serves two.

Buck's Quick Tips: Horseradish is an acceptable condiment but horse apples are not.

Regional variations for the last roundup include Filly Gumbo in New Orleans and Charlie's Trotter Tenders in Chicago.

High horse ownership in Texas provides the largest opportunity for a personal Daily Double.

If a horse owner sees you tip over his or her stakes contender, you'll experience your very own "Most Exciting Two Minutes in Road Sports."

Trust Buck. Not every horse you purchase on your race through the horse acre communities will be a Thoroughbred.

A regular diet of horse meat will provide the necessary giddyup and go for any activity.

Horsemeat with an Asian Flair: Basashi (Sushi)

1 pound horse fillet

1 cup soy sauce

½ cup onions

¼ cup pickled ginger

1 teaspoon wasabi

Cut and trim the horsemeat into thin slices. In a mixing bowl, combine the soy sauce, onions, ginger, and wasabi. Dip the strips in the bowl and make sure the meat is sufficiently covered. Serves two.

Buck's Quick Tips: The primary symptom of *basashi* overdose is to count by tapping your feet.

The chefs at the Polo Lounge recommend mixing 1 pound of pork to every 2 pounds of polo horse meat to be really sure.

The best cuts on a New York City police horse are not available at the precinct level.

Naughty zebras are released in the zoo's big cat cages 1 hour after visiting hours.

The steaks under the saddle of most circus ponies are the toughest, even more so on the Shetland owned by the singing fat lady.

The cafeterias of major U.S. veterinary schools are the most reliable places to enjoy horse meat. For that matter, cat and dog meat, too.

Testicle Festival

Summers are full of fairs and festivals for the whole family. Any serious roadside shopper would be nuts to miss the annual Testicle Festival held midsummer in Clinton, Montana. Similar though smaller fund-raising events are scattered around the country, but the Big Sky party is a really big ball. The cojone camaraderie will introduce you to an unexpected culinary universe.

Tasty Tidbits from Under a Buck

Rocky Mountain, or prairie oysters—originally only the testicles of lambs and calves—are low-hanging fruit for the roadside shopper. Preparations of such campfire delicacies have progressed from being tossed in the fire pit at branding time, retrieved, peeled, and enjoyed al dente. Basque shepherds have a reputation of removing oysters with their teeth—yet another reason to drop their daughters at the curb.

Nuts were used in the original Waldorf salad. Harvard researchers have found that women who eat nuts have a lower risk of type 2 diabetes than non-nut eaters. Walnuts, almonds, peanuts, and cashews are mentioned as alternatives.

For additional testicle recipes, see Lesbian Wedding Receptions (page 252).

2 pounds large animal testicles

4 cups extra-virgin olive or peanut oil

2 eggs, beaten

1 cup cornmeal or seasoned all-purpose flour

Hot pepper jelly

Clean and skin the testicles. Heat the oil to 350°F. Slice or butterfly the testicles, dip in the egg, and roll in the cornmeal. Deep-fry in the oil until golden brown and serve with the jelly. Serves four nutcases.

VARIATION: Slice clean and skinned testicles into ½-inch-thick rounds and soak in beer for a couple of hours. Remove from the beer and pat dry, dip in beaten egg, and roll in panko. Deep-fry in extra-virgin olive oil until golden brown and serve while singing the following:

Sellin' nuts, hot nuts, anybody here want to buy my nuts?

Sellin' nuts, hot nuts, I've got nuts for sale.

You tell me that man's nuts is mighty small,

Best to have small nuts than no nuts at all

Selling nuts, hot nuts, you buy 'em from the peanut man!

–Lil Johnson, 1935

Port is the perfect accompaniment for roasted nuts, and even an average ruby port will display a nutty character of its own. A measure of respect for the donor is to match the maturity of the port with the age of the nut-sack twins: a fresh two-year-old port for a young whitetail buck's contribution, and a late-bottled tawny port for accidental interaction with a large ungulate in a national park.

Buck's Quick Tips: A properly prepared tanned nut-sack from a large animal is an original gift for all ages, from children to put their marbles in to a mother-in-law who frequently loses hers. The choices for nut-sacks are with hair on or off, and the most efficient nut-sacks are made with a rawhide drawstring.

The original intention of gelding or castrating cattle, pigs, and sheep was to make the males more manageable. With the exception of anecdotal evidence heard in divorce courts, the procedure has limited human appeal. However, choir directors always have room in the upper bleachers for one more castrati.

Castrati are not eunuchs. Eunuchs are married men whose spouses out-weigh them by at least two to one.

What's the difference between beer nuts and deer nuts? The latter are under a buck. Harrumph, wheeze, kack, oops, sorry, didn't mean to spit.

Game Day

In the fall, AFL and NFL leagues roll from their training camps and fill Saturday and Sunday afternoons with plenty of family room and stadium action. It's time to roll out your favorite wild Game Day party snacks.

Other than beer nuts and deep-fried deer nuts (see Testicle Festival, page 87) on Saturdays, hot wings are a staple at the Valhalla Lounge in Buck's Wilderness Lodge. The origin of hot wings is claimed by Buffalo, New York. Everyone but the town idiot in Buffalo, Wyoming, knows buffalo don't have wings, unless one in Yellowstone chases you.

Chicken wings are used in most commercial Buffalo wings, but active road shoppers, particularly in the Midwest, prefer upland bird wings. A fat ring-necked pheasant is the bird of choice, and quail, grouse, and doves are suitable for smaller bites. If you want to make it personal for the birdbrains on the opposing team, use ravens, falcons, and cardinals. With these smaller birds, you'll never be short a toothpick.

Wild Wings

12 pheasant wings

4 tablespoons extra-virgin olive oil

2 tablespoons garlic salt

Dipping sauces: barbecue sauce, blue cheese salad dressing, jalapeño-infused sour cream, and flavored yogurt

Preheat the oven to 400°F. Place the wings on a baking sheet lined with foil. Brush the wings with the oil and season with the garlic salt. Bake for 35 to 40 minutes, until tender. Serve with celery sticks and dipping sauces.

For neigh-sayers, a horse haunch will roil the cowboys in Denver and Indianapolis.

Tailgate Chili

There is no more heartwarming meal on a cool, crisp autumn afternoon than a hot, steaming bowl of wild game chili. Chili can be prepared in advance of your meat purchase and has so many variations that every appetite can be satisfied. Everyone, even chili lovers not yet born, has their own "original," "true," or "authentic" version (beans, no beans, beef, no beef). The following is guaranteed to fire your team spirit:

3 tablespoons extra-virgin olive oil

½ pound red ground round

½ pound bacon, chopped

½ cup chopped onion

4 tablespoons vinegar

½ cup brown sugar

½ cup ketchup

1 (15-ounce) can kidney beans, undrained

1 (15-ounce) can butter beans, drained

1 (28-ounce) can B&M® beans

Preheat the oven to 350°F. In a skillet, heat the oil over medium-high heat and brown the ground round, bacon, and onions separately. Combine with the remaining ingredients in a bean pot, cover, and bake for 2 hours. Serves four.

If your team is playing the Buffalo Bills, chunks of buffalo will fit the bill. When the Minnesota Golden Gophers are the opposition, add chunks of that striped dog to the pot. As the Chicago Bears line up across the field, don't forget, "Only you can prevent forest fires."

Buck's Quick Tip: An upland game bird the size of the San Diego chicken will feed the entire home and away teams.

Holidays

Groundhog Day

Groundhog Day celebrates that fat vegetable garden thief coming out of his hole after a seasonal snooze to look for his shadow. As the story goes, if he sees his shadow on February 2, he figures six more weeks of bad weather are coming and returns to his long winter nap, leaving behind the most troubling groundhog thoughts: Where is Phat Phil's missus? Is Punxsutawney Phyllis living in domestic terror? Should a marriage counselor be sent down the hole? Donations to Buck, in care of the publisher, will go for an intervention.

Groundhogs are also called woodchucks, of "How much wood would a woodchuck upchuck if he was held upside down and shaken real hard by a Chamber of Commerce director?" fame. These large rodents enjoy too favorable media attention and any roadside shopper out hog-hunting strikes a blow for better TV, whatever better TV is.

Ground Groundhog

1 pound ground round groundhog

1 egg, lightly beaten

¼ cup bread crumbs

1 teaspoon cracked red pepper

1 clove garlic, crushed

1 small white onion, minced

If your ground round is not ground finely enough, cut it into 1-inch cubes and run through a meat grinder with a medium blade. Slip in a couple of pieces of smoked thick-sliced bacon at the same time, for flavor.

Prepare a grill. Combine all the ingredients and form into 4 patties. Grill, flipping only once. Serves four.

Buck's Quick Tips: Groundhog tastes somewhere between a squirrel and a raccoon, with a hint of field mouse.

Phat Philly Cheesesteak Sandwich: Thinly slice a pound of this fat darling and fry in extra-virgin olive oil until medium-rare. Add caramelized onions and a few green bell pepper slices. Divide among 4 kaiser buns and cover with Cheez Whiz®.

Easter

Here comes Peter Cottontail

Hopping down the bunny trail.

Hippity-hoppity, hippity-hoppity

Dinner's on its way.

For many shoppers, Easter is a celebration of the arrival of Peter Cottontail and the spring harvest of Farmer McGregor's garden. Peter so loves Farmer McGregor's fresh carrots and, in his silly mind, he thinks the fresh greens should belong to everyone in the fuzzy-wuzzy woods.

Peter has to cross busy Main Street to visit Farmer McGregor's garden. Given the high cost of political posturing, the local PETA chapter hasn't been able to provide a safe cross-hop for woodland animals. Peter must cross during the most dangerous periods, in the early morning and at dusk, when Peter's mom and dad are making baby rabbits in the warren master bedroom.

Petered-Out Rabbit

Rabbit has been unfairly promoted as stew meat for years. Old recipes called for rabbit pieces to be boiled in water or canned chicken broth (can you imagine how disrespectful this is to Peter?) and white wine until almost done, and then everything in the produce section is thrown into the pot (even frozen vegetables) until really done. Bon appétit.

Before cooking, skin and clean freshly acquired bunny rabbit, and remove the head and unlucky rabbit feet. Field bunnies can carry a disease called tularemia, but cooking kills the bacteria. Check for white spots on the liver.

OPTION 1: IN THE FIELD

Wash the rabbit carefully and pat dry. Prepare an open fire. Secure the rabbit to a long stick and roast over the fire until done.

OPTION 2: AT HOME

Wash the rabbit carefully and pat dry. Preheat the oven to 325°F. Split the rabbit into two halves, rub with extra-virgin olive oil, and season with black pepper. Place in a baking pan and bake for 30 minutes, or until brown. Serves two.

Buck's Quick Tips: If you are late for the Easter Morning parade, no worry. Parents buy rabbits for their irresponsible young as pets, and two weeks later they are released into the wild because they acted like rabbits.

There is scant anecdotal evidence of rabbit meat's acting as an aphrodisiac. However, early church documents do forbid young priests from observing rabbit rituals.

Cottontails don't really have tails made of cotton. They have little value as swabs, but a high ornamental value for party clothing.

Who said rabbit feet bring good luck? Peter had four!

For Buck's renowned recipe for *Hasenpflatten*, locate a collector's copy of *Buck Peterson's International Roadkill Cookbook* and turn to page 61.

Editor's Note: Apologies to the Beatrix Pothead estate for intermingling the bunny stories. They weren't true anyway.

Buck's Welsh Rabbit

For those who cried during the movie Miss Potter, *Buck's Welsh Rabbit will soothe their bruised nerves.*

**¾ pound cheddar cheese, grated
(the more English and more aged, the better)**

¼ cup ale

½ teaspoon dry mustard

½ teaspoon kosher salt

2 tablespoons unsalted butter

1 teaspoon Worcestershire sauce

In a saucepan over medium heat, combine the ingredients and stir until you have a smooth sauce. Pour over toasted (or grilled like a panini for tire-track authenticity) whole wheat bread and serve. Serves four. You are welcome.

St. Patrick's Day

St. Patrick's Day is celebrated in America on March 17, a feast honoring the patron saint of Ireland. St. Patrick had only one son, Danny Boy, whose pipes were always calling from glen to glen, and down the mountainside to the annoyance of nearby goat herders. The 35 million Americans that claim Irish ancestry mark the holiday with traditional homeland fare and individual 55-gallon drums of green beer.

In their native land, the Irish exposure to road shopping is limited to a few gray squirrels, long-tailed field mice, and the odd badger. Too many people watch the small red deer population to build a sustainable road harvest. The most common Irish meal ingredient is the potato, yet the

Irish potato can hardly be classified as a game vegetable, as potatoes don't migrate south for the winter, have lengthy courtships between the male and female, or occupy an easily identifiable place in the food chain, with the notable exception of Polish vodka. Second- and third-generation Irish families recall the early hard days of following a bouncing landlord's cart for a wild tuber, and the traditional preparation survives in American homes.

Highway Smashed Browns

8 small- to medium-size potatoes (red preferred)

½ cup extra-virgin olive oil

½ cup grated cheese

Wash the dirt from the potatoes and cover with cold water in a 3-quart pot. Add a tablespoon of salt to keep your sodium content high. Boil until almost soft–around 12 minutes–drain and smash whatever isn't smashed. In a skillet, heat the oil over medium-high heat and transfer the potatoes to the skillet, Cook on slightly lower heat, turning until they are golden brown (less than 30 minutes). Sprinkle with cheese and serve hot. Your guests will kiss your Blarney Stone. Serves twelve, the average-size Irish family.

Buck's Quick Tips: A toast is appropriate to herald these servings. Among the Irish favorites:

> May you be in heaven half an hour before
> the Devil knows you're dead.

> May you always have a large russet to put in the
> front of your bathing suit on a beach holiday.

The patron saint of the potato, Saint Ore-Ida, is rarely seen in Irish churches.

Corned Carnage and Cabbage

A St. Patrick's Day meal with meat is the traditional Irish stew or corned beef with cabbage. The amount of lamb in the stew signified prosperity and was covered by potatoes, turnips, parsnips, and leeks from any taxmen lurking in the neighborhood. The latter dish is Irish America's embrace of the inexpensive beef brisket, but for our purposes, we'll revive the use of badger brisket. Wisconsin Badgers are the favorites in the fall, until the Minnesota Gophers find a better quarterback.

CORNED CARNAGE:

4 pounds badger meat, skinned

⅓ cup kosher salt

3 bay leaves

1 tablespoon ground black pepper

2 teaspoons mustard seeds

2 teaspoons paprika

2 teaspoons dried thyme

2 teaspoons ground allspice

1 teaspoon ground coriander

1 teaspoon ground cloves

Make sure the fur is removed from the meat and stab every side with a sharp, pointy knife several times. In a spice or coffee mill, combine the remaining ingredients and grind to a powder. Massage the mixture evenly into the meat and place in a 1-gallon resealable plastic bag. Make sure no air has been left in the bag, seal, and place in a baking pan. Use a weight (steam iron or bowling ball) to press down the meat. Refrigerate for 5 days, turning once a day.

CARNAGE AND CABBAGE:

1 recipe Corned Carnage (above)

3 cups chicken stock

1 head cabbage, quartered

Preheat the oven to 225°F. Wash the spices off the meat and place in a baking pan with a lid, along with the stock. Cover and roast for 3½ hours. Add the cabbage and roast for another 20 minutes, or until the cabbage is done. Slice the meat and serve with Irish soda bread. Serves eight.

Buck's Quick Tip: Pinching a young Irish lass's butt is more likely to be tolerated on this holiday, especially if her priest and cop brothers aren't around.

Cinco de Mayo

The Fifth of May celebration in the United States commemorates the Mexican army's unexpected victory over larger, better-equipped French forces at the Battle of Puebla in 1862. It's not clear why France invaded Mexico, but locals say it had something to do with a secret molé sauce.

Cinco de Mayo is not a federal holiday even in Mexico, but fervently celebrated in the United States by distributors of Corona, Dos Equis, Pacifica, Tecate, Carta Blanca, Modelo Especial, and other libations that go well with free bar nachos. Not to mention the appreciation of the Lime Growers Federation and salt farmers.

The list of Cinco de Mayo food favorites is long, yet most are quick and easy to make. The most popular meal is also the simplest to prepare.

TACOS

Taco comes from the ancient Mexican word *ac*, meaning "flat." This is from Nahuatl chefs pounding fresh masa with their foreheads.

Food fashions du jour, like the *torta*, have had their five minutes of fame, but the taco remains supreme forever. The key to a well-made taco is to be creative in the individual layers. As you might suspect, road shopping creates culinary artists.

Tortilla: A taco is a tortilla wrapped around filling. Corn tortillas are more common in Mexico; flour tortillas are preferred north of the Rio Grande. Soft flour and hard-shell corn tortillas are supermarket staples and should be part of any roadside shopper's basket. Fried tacos are the most interesting variation; the contrast of crunchy shell to soft, moist filling is much like biting into a deep-fried squirrel head.

Meat: Any meat can be used in the first layer of the filling. The most popular taco in Mexico is the *taco al pastor*, made of spiced pork sliced from a gyro-style meat log. Road shoppers use any daily special, including meats that slither and rattle across the roadway. In the north, garden snakes are the most common road occupants (but Buck has a magnificent bull snake framed above the fireplace), and in the southwest, rattlesnake is the daily special. The rattle makes a nice toy for the youngsters.

Tex-Mess Taco

1 corn or flour tortilla

1 snake loin, roasted and chopped

1 handful lettuce, chopped

1 tomato, sliced

Cheese, shredded (or substitute cheese in a can)

Holding the tortilla in your left hand, stuff with the snake loin and top with the lettuce, tomato, and cheese. Fold the tortilla in half and enjoy. Serves one.

Boulevard Burrito

1 (12-inch) flour or corn tortilla

Rice, cooked

Black beans, cooked

Snake loin, roasted and chopped

Salsa

Cheese, shredded (or substitute cheese in a can)

Sour cream

Guacamole (optional)

Layer the tortilla with a stretch of rice and black beans, add a healthy dollop of snake loin, top with salsa, shredded cheese, and sour cream (guacamole optional–gives author the squirts), and fold the ends in. Roll the tortilla and wrap in foil. The torpedo can now be thrown across the room to an eager eater. Serves one.

Buck's Quick Tip: Guacamole (from *guaca*–green caca, and *molé*– dark baby poop) should only be used with caution.

Tarmac Taco Salad

1 head lettuce, chopped

4 tomatoes, chopped

1 bunch green onions, chopped

4 ounces sharp cheddar cheese, grated

8 ounces Thousand Island dressing

½ (14½-ounce) bag Doritos® Nacho Cheese

1 pound red ground round

Salt and ground black pepper

1 (14-ounce) can red kidney beans, drained

In a serving bowl, combine the tomatoes, lettuce, green onions, cheese, and Thousand Island dressing. Mix well. Break but do not crush the tortilla chips and add to mixture. In a skillet, brown the meat, season with salt and pepper, add the kidney beans, and cook until the beans are tender. Let cool and stir into the salad mixture, and be prepared to make more. Serves six to eight.

Buck's Quick Tips: Space limitations do not allow us to reprint the recipe for Burro Bourguignon, but this famous equestrian dish can be found in Julio y Julia's classic, *Mastering the Art of Mexican Cooking*, page 45 of the English edition.

The ASPCA warns that homemade piñatas constructed of deceased road mammals is prohibited.

Father's Day

The first Father's Day was celebrated in 1910 through the efforts of a Spokane, Washington, woman named Sonora Smart Dodd, but it wasn't until President Lyndon Johnson declared it a federal holiday in 1966 that greeting card companies started chopping down old-growth timber. Father's Day is held on the third Sunday of June and Unknown Father's Day is acknowledged whenever the child support check finally arrives. Traditional Father's Day celebrations are based around a special meal for dear old Dad. Truth be told, Dad's favorite is when Mom relinquishes control of the kitchen.

Road-Salted Rib Eye

Most serious carnivores considered the rib eye to be the best steak in the road. In northern climates, roadside rib eyes arrive preseasoned with a salt crust provided by the winter road crews. Rib eyes are the end of the rib roast and have neither an eye nor a rib; a more accurate description would be a ribless, eyeless steak.

1 large, 1½-inch-thick venison steak, taken from a one-year-old dry whitetail doe that lived near a cornfield

2 tablespoons extra-virgin olive oil

Salt and ground black pepper

Warning: If you like your steak medium to well done, give the meat to a homeless person, a neighbor's dog, anyone, or anything. You don't deserve it. And read no further.

Wash, scrub, and dig out any remaining road salt from the meat, especially crew-applied salt mixed with sand. Brush both sides with oil and dust with salt and pepper. Preheat a cast-iron skillet to medium-high heat. Place the steak in the pan and turn after 2½ minutes to cook the other side. Remove the steak from the pan and let rest for 3 to 5 minutes (this allows the juices inside to settle down). Season lightly and serve.

VARIATION: Sear both sides of the meat in a very hot pan and bake in a 500°F oven for 2½ minutes. Remove the meat and let sit for 3 to 5 minutes. Either way, this Father's Day meal is ready in less than 10 minutes.

Buck's Quick Tip: No need to rely on county trucks to salt your fillets. Gourmet salts can be found in large city supermarkets and online. Choices range from kosher salt to mesquite-smoked sea salt to pink salt mined in the Himalayas. Don't quibble like the salt snots on when to add salt: twenty-four hours before, just before cooking, during, and/or after cooking. Use your remaining taste buds to decide. Be sure to throw a pinch of table salt over your left shoulder for game warden–free shopping.

Fourth of July

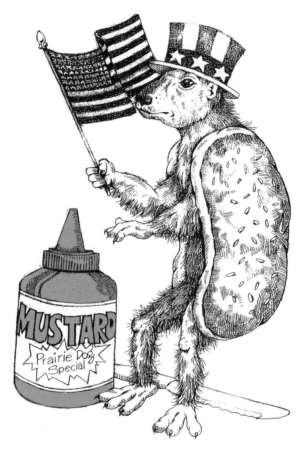

What better way to celebrate our nation's birthday than with a hot dog fresh off the grill? Buck's favorite shopping areas for the main ingredients are the large prairie dog towns near Glenrock, Wyoming, where ranchers appreciate your removal of these ankle-busting hole diggers. Other fine canine supermarkets are scattered throughout the western states and the Dakotas. There is probably no better way to declare your independence from the tasteless supermarket dogs, and celebrate your new position of top dog on the prairie.

Top Dog
(American Mashed Banger)

According to the National Hot Dog and Sausage Council, Americans eat 150 million hot dogs on Independence Day. Those dogs are full of nitrites and nitrates to improve their color and extend shelf life. Prairie dogs are nitrite/nitrate free and, commercial claims to the contrary, grass fed and free range.

1 prairie dog

1 foot-long hot dog bun

Ketchup

Dijon mustard, or your choice

Prepare a grill. Gut, skin, and clean the dog (every dog lover knows skinless hot dogs are easier to bite into). Place the dog on the grill and cook over medium heat until heated through, turning occasionally. The internal temperature should be 160°F. Place the dog in the bun and garnish with mustard and ketchup to taste. Serves one.

VARIATIONS:

Detroit: Place the cooked dog in a grilled bun and cover with canned chili, diced onions, and shredded cheddar cheese. A Motor City favorite.

Kansas City: Place the cooked dog in a sesame- or poppy-seed bun and top with melted Swiss cheese and sauerkraut. "What's up, dog? How's your bro, Reuben?"

Chicago: Place the cooked dog in a poppy-seed bun and top with chopped onion, tomato slices, spicy pickled green peppers, relish, yellow mustard, a pickle spear, and a pinch of celery salt.

Los Angeles: Korean street dogs are topped with kimchi, made from shredded and fermented cabbage. A variation of the South of the Border (below) is a bacon-wrapped dog covered with a spicy sauce of onions, tomatoes, mustard, mayonnaise, ketchup, and spices, and topped with a large poblano chile pepper. Whoah!

New York: Sidewalk vendors add brown mustard and onions stewed in tomato sauce. Do not tip them unless you want to doom the vendors to a life of codependency.

Atlanta: Top a cooked small-plot garden dog with coleslaw, baked beans, ketchup, mustard, chili, and onions.

South of the Border: Wrap the dog in bacon strips (like a barber pole) before roasting and wrap in a corn or flour tortilla. Top with chopped onions and sliced tomatoes, and squirt a line of salsa. Olé!

Buck's Quick Tip: A staple state- and county-fair food, the corn dog is nothing but a regular dog that is coated in cornmeal batter and deep-fried. The name comes from its resemblance to an ear of corn when cooked, but Midwesterners say it looks more like a marsh cattail. National Corndog Day also happens to coincide with NCAA March Madness. If you have the opportunity to purchase a whole family during the dog days of summer, Hushed Puppies redefine and refresh the art of cornmeal dumplings. For urban dogs, substitute 2 pounds of cubed waterfront dog for the eggplant in any ratatouille recipe for a protein-fueled Ratatat-touille.

For the authentic corned dog, see Corned Carnage and Cabbage (page 101).

Thanksgiving

Almost 90 percent of Americans eat domestic turkey for Thanksgiving. The other 10 percent prefer meat with flavor, which brings us to the wild road bird. This is great news for roadside shoppers, as wild turkey population growth in the United States has been dramatic. There is little reason to put a domestic turkey in front of family and friends when five large subspecies of gobblers are running loose.

The eastern subspecies offers over 5 million shopping opportunities and they are the largest of the wily birds, weighing over 20 pounds. Although this bird is found east of the Mississippi, West Coast transplants can be run over as well. The Rio Grande subspecies offers a fifth of the opportunities as the eastern, but the market is always open for western drivers. The Florida-only Osceola is a tough bird to bag and they inhabit areas where giant hogs live. Knocking down a Merriam's and the Gould's subspecies would, in all of the five subspecies, be considered a roadside shopper's Grand Slam.

A perfectly acceptable substitute is heritage turkeys wandering on hobby farms. Heritage turkeys are the ancestors of the common broad-breasted white domestic turkey with the built-in red "It's done" belly button. Heritage turkeys taste better. If the opportunity presents itself, pilgrim, tip over a big Bourbon Red or Narragansett.

Buck's Quick Tip: The old tom is preferred for its weight and meat texture; young toms can be tough. In reverse, young hens are preferred over old hens. This is also a reasonable dating principle.

Turnkey Turkey

1 pound wild turkey breasts, pounded into cutlets

3 tablespoons extra-virgin olive oil

⅓ cup nuts, finely chopped: pecans, almonds, or walnuts (not testicles, you nut job)

In a skillet, warm half the oil over medium-high heat. Coat the cutlets with the remaining oil and coat with the nuts. Place the cutlets in the pan and lower the heat slightly. Cook each side for 5 minutes, or until golden brown. Serves four turkey meat gobblers when accompanied with Roasted Road Russets (page 33).

Save turkey testicles for a late-night snack. For vegetarians, the testicles are part of the gobbler's package.

Bonus Big Bird Preparation

Preheat the oven to 350°F. Clean, wash, and pat dry a whole bird. Salt and pepper the cavity and fill with your favorite dressing. Roast uncovered for 3 hours, basting every 15 minutes with melted butter. Check the doneness with a meat thermometer. Let rest for 15 minutes. Serves six.

Buck's Quick Tips: Both sexes in industrial domestic turkey production live in the henhouse, a situation that mimics much of domestic suburbia. According to the USDA's food safety agency, free-range domestic turkeys must have access to the outdoors. It's not clear if the access is just a dirty window. The turkeys must be available for injections of salted butter, water, edible fats, and other flavor enhancers.

Benjamin Franklin argued for the wild turkey as our national symbol, but this was after he had been hit in the head by lightning and started to call himself Little Richard. The National White Taste-Free Turkey Foundation still contributes a small stipend to the Ben Franklin Foundation. The other bird under consideration was the bald eagle; most Native Americans agree the golden eagle tastes better.

Christmas

The National Highway Safety Council estimates over 750,000 deer-car interactions a year, and the number is also an approximation of the annual road harvest. The majority of way-up-close encounters take place in the late fall and early winter, when the attentions of whitetail deer in particular turn to romance. Venison, the king of wild game meat, is available for the most festive holiday of the year. Ho, ho, ho!

Your holiday house will clear of family and friends when you start slicing Bambi into steaks. Use this time to eat as many huge or multiple small venison steaks before the ingrates return. Since you're in command, take advantage of the functionality of Buck's dream kitchen (see page 119).

I'm Dreaming of a
Whitetail Christmas

6 (1½-inch-thick) venison steaks

5 tablespoons unsalted butter

1 tablespoon ground black pepper

3 large heads garlic, halved

1 cup pheasant broth

1 tablespoon extra-virgin olive oil

Salt

½ cup dry red wine

1 cup water

Preheat the oven to 350°F. Make sure every bit of fur and road tar has been removed from the meat and set aside. In a skillet, melt the butter over medium-high heat. Pepper the garlic and place cut side down in the skillet. Add the broth, cover, and simmer until tender. Uncover and continue simmering until the liquid is reduced by half. Remove the garlic and set aside. In another skillet, heat the oil over high heat. Salt and pepper the steaks and sear for 2 minutes. Set aside the steaks, pour the wine into a skillet, and reduce by half. Add the water and reduce again by half. Remove from the heat, add the remaining butter, and pour over the steaks. Top with the garlic halves. Serves Buck nicely.

VARIATIONS: Venison is the most forgiving wild game meat. Wild deer meat can be braised, boiled, deep-fried, breaded, roasted, chopped up for tacos and tamales and *tortas*, ground into burger, and still think highly of you. Venison chunks destined for stew are better served in a Midwestern hot dish. In a casserole dish, combine a pound of browned ground road venison, 1 can of mushroom soup, 1 can of cream of chicken soup, 1 cup of water, 1½ cups of cooked wild rice (from Big Babe Lake), sliced mushrooms, finely chopped celery, and a shot of hot sauce. Bake at 350°F for 30 minutes, covered, and then uncover and bake for 30 minutes more. Burp!

Trim 1-inch-thin pieces for a venison stroganoff that will curl your toes. Brown the venison pieces in unsalted butter, add sliced mushrooms and a sliced small onion, cook over medium heat until the onion is tender, and set aside. In the same skillet, melt several tablespoons of butter and add the juices from the previous pan-fry, meat, vegetables, 1 cup of sour cream, and 1 tablespoon of sherry, and stir slowly so the mixture is evenly heated. Serve over wild rice and tell the pleading canine face under the table, "You haven't been that good this year." Happy holidays from the host of Christmas presents!!

Odds and Ends

Buck's Dream Kitchen

Buck's kitchen on Whitetail Ridge is, unlike most culinary magazine recommendations, well within the budget of most roadside shoppers. The key features of Buck's kitchen (left to right):

1. The lever-action carbine on the wall changes by season: a Marlin Model 39A 22 for small game and a pre-1964 Winchester Model 94 30-30 for big game when the shopping cart is having its bumper repaired. Grenade launchers for dangerous game are in the study.

2. The meat diagram works for all mammals. Visiting vegetarians are told that mammals normally have feet and a head. Birds don't need a diagram and are plucked in the yard and, if needed, breasted in the mudroom through the curtained back door.

3. Knives include an 8-inch all-purpose blade, a #7 Shrade Uncle Henry® fillet knife, a CUTCO® 4½-inch serrated knife for really tough testicles, and a large SOG® throwing knife to enforce kitchen discipline and preserve decorum.

4. A gimbal hanging from the ceiling is used to finish carving what was started on the shoulder of the road, and can be lifted or lowered according to the size of the purchase. The saw does what the knife selection can't. A cutting board replaces the drip pan once the premium cuts are made. Scraps are shoved off the end of the table for the miniature dachshund and Blue Healer guard dogs.

5. Adult beverages are shared by hardworking kitchen help, with the smallest shot glasses used in the beginning of the evening. Yukon Jack® is the preferred beverage for slicing and dicing a moose, while listening to Robert Service's Yukon stories on the new Bose® radio.

6. The stove hasn't worked for years, so a fire with fatback wood is used to whip up a Quick-Fix steak. The exhaust fan is strong enough to lift Buck out of his easy chair.

7. The sink has an industrial-strength garbage disposal unit rated to grind most large bones and small skulls.

8. In season, the windows are covered with heavy plastic so game wardens and nosy neighbors cannot see in. The plastic covering is secured on the outside with inexpensive 1-inch wood lath.

9. The refrigerator is professional quality and adjacent to a walk-in cooler with industrial-strength exhaust fans for the kitchen help's use of medical marijuana.

10. The condiments include pepper jelly for fried rabbit livers.

A Short Wine Primer—
What Every Quick-Fix Chef
Needs to Know

A glass of wine with a meal can lower your risk of heart disease, especially if you consider how many meals you can enjoy in a single day. Don't forget Sunday brunch. A nice glass of wine can aid in digestion and, as noted below, lower your risk of a broken heart.

Recent research indicates that light to moderate drinking (1 to 28 drinks per week) reduces the risk of dementia in male drinkers by 45 percent and in women by 27 percent. The study wasn't clear if women could further lower their risk by moving from moderate to tailgate-style drinking (29 to 290 drinks per week).

You'll know when you've properly matched a wine with a road food. Your friends take your car keys and you sleep on the couch.

Guide to Alcohol Content

It takes three 6-ounce servings of 8 percent–alcohol wine for an average-size woman and a thimble full for a bulimic fashion model to entertain one of your dating suggestions.

It takes two 6-ounce servings of 16 percent–alcohol wine for that same average woman to entertain several of your suggestions and retain the ability to crawl out the ladies' room window.

Order bigger (boozier) wines to tip over any remaining moral objections.

Roadkill Wine Pairing

One of the reasons why some drivers hesitate to include roadkill in their daily meals is the uncertainty as to which wine to pair with which critter.

Wine pairing by the time of day: breakfast at dawn, midmorning snack, noon lunch, midafternoon snack, and tapas and dinner out on the deck with cigars at dusk. Start the day with a sparkling wine for breakfast and end with a bold, fruit-forward red with high alcohol content.

WINE PAIRING BY ANIMAL PURCHASED

Most of the recipes in this book are for red meat. You can't go wrong with a Pinot Noir for subtler meats such as whitetail fawn, a tannin-rich Cabernet and Bordeaux for elk and dark meats such as bear and road-aged meats, and a fruity white for road pork and upland birds.

WINE PAIRING BY ANIMAL PART

Wine writers under deadline will pair adjectives with food nouns: a brisk Pinot with elk brisket, an earthy Shiraz for dirt-covered road meat, a sweet rosé with sweetbreads, and a balls-to-the-wall Chardonnay with almond overtones to be served with testicles. Disregard their blather. Trust only Buck and continue reading.

WINE PAIRING BY RECIPE

Spicy foods, even barbecue, deserve a Malbec or a good Shiraz. Sweet-and-sour pork ears or snouts need a dry Riesling, and ginger-infused possum cheeks call for a fruity Gewürztraminer. For offal, pair with a decent Zinfandel and/or a strong mouthwash between servings.

Building Your Own Wine Collection

Build a life list of the bottles you've known. Use a portion of your family budget for nonmeritorious wines, wines that have lost their labels and are sitting in a marked-down grocery cart. Or go crazy trying to sift through the oenophile babble for a good buy.

SET A BUDGET

Wine purchases should not exceed a certain percentage of your monthly mortgage payment, 25 to 30 percent for most singles and 15 to 20 percent for most alcoholic couples. Pick a number and stick to it.

SHOP NONTRADITIONAL OUTLETS

Catholic Church supply houses are reliable sources for inexpensive bulk wines. Follow the priest on his Saturday rounds for the nearest locations.

Wine Storage

Box wines should be stored in such a way that the spigot doesn't dry out. Boxes are easier to store on a shelf in the garage than bottles are, and compressed boxes take up less room in the recycle bin.

Roadkill Wineglasses

The obsession of wine snots to match the perfect wine with the perfect food is continued in the selection of wineglasses. Dear reader, take it from Buck, there is no such thing as the perfect container to serve wine. Glass manufacturers try to persuade the unwary to purchase official sizes, shapes, colors, and capacities. Oenophiles drone on about the legs swirled on the inner wall of a glass and the nose of an overpriced wine delivered by the shape of a tulip glass. The tulip shape is thought to deliver the most intense sniff and is the easiest to swirl 'n' swig.

A WINEGLASS PRIMER

Traditional wineglasses have three parts—the bulb, the stem, and the foot. The most important part is the bulb—the wine container. The stem must be tall enough for the size of your paw as you lift the wine to judge and mumble nonsense about its color and clarity. And, of course, the foot

must be large enough so the bulb, filled to the top, doesn't tip over when a llama or, worse, a faux French waiter backs into your table.

Red wine glasses are most easily identified in the Wine-Tasting Room in Buck's Culinary Institute by the red residue on the bottom of the bulb. Elsewhere, red wine glasses are typically a larger size compared to white wine glasses.

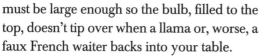

White wine glasses are characterized by the smaller size compared to red wine glasses and cost roughly the same.

Wine bars like smaller glasses; smaller amounts look larger, influencing the tip jar.

The wineglasses in the Valhalla Wine and Tapas Bar in Buck's Lodge on Big Babe Lake are most familiar to those who frequent English pubs.

Ye Olde Yard of Wine® glass holds about 40 ounces (8 standard glasses) of wine and is favored by regulars who appreciate not having to go to the bar for a refill. The bouquet of your favorite vintage is concentrated in this tower of grape power and the wide opening evokes fond memories of Schmidt's Big Mouth. Individuals of less lusty appetites choose the Ye Olde Half a Yard® or Ye Olde Foot®.

Cooking with Wine

Cooking with wine comes under the general category of cooking with alcohol. Due to space restrictions, Buck has left cooking with hard liquor and other alcohol-based liquids such as lighter fluid and used jet fuel to others.

Wine is used for Quick-Fix road meats in braising and, if time allows, marinating a tough piece. What wine to use? No worry; use whatever is handy, the half-empty bottles from the last party, or a bottle of Lancer's or Mateus from Grandmother's private stash.

Buck's House Wine

Buck's house wine is Minnesota's most layered Syrah and the product of wine-making's oldest tradition: fruit hand picked by defrocked priests, foot stomped by humans not Sonoma llamas; red oak wood presses; and corks made from old U.S. Navy life preservers. All in the service of a subtle, complex fruit bomb.

The grape was selected to complement many of the red meats found in northern climates such as Buck's home base. Subtle flavors of blackberry, chokecherry, blueberry, and dingleberry with a hint of baby loon droppings enchant the experienced and enthuse the novice, especially when served in Ye Olde Yard of Wine®.

The macroclimate of Buck's private wine-growing area is characterized by warm summer days, swarming mosquitoes and black flies at the lake, and cool nights with no-see-ums undeterred by vintage Shell No-Pest Strips. The vineyard's sandy soil with iron ore tailings provides essential minerals and a warm cast of fall colors when spilled on a white carpet. The finish is surprisingly crisp, with a deer bed vibrancy that lingers on the educated palate.

The more powerful Syrah grape is matched perfectly with the more delicate Shiraz grape, infusing the nose with fruit preferred by the black bear, and hints of black peppercorn, Alaskan muskeg, a pinch of Skoal Mint Long Cut®, and a fried Spam® sandwich.

Buck's wine is an excellent choice for all red meats as is, or watered down 20 to 30 percent for upland birds and other light-colored meats, not to mention french fries.

A big-hearted red perfectly matched to venison hung over a bumper from Nevis to Minneapolis.

—Johnny Yuma, the Wine Rebel

Aromas of acorns roasted over a forest fire fill the well-poured glass.

—Robert Parker, *The Other White Whiner*

I like to swirl the wine. But not too much because it reminds me of when I got sick on the Tilt-a-Whirl and threw up cotton candy and tiny doughnuts on my mom.

—Chastity Bumbottom

Buck's Syrah has more notes than Freddy Fender singing "Wasted Days, Wasted Nights."

—Wickiphobia

The first sniff of this Syrah screams northern Minnesota and the third week in deer camp.

—Edgar Humperdink, 7-Eleven Corporate Sommelier

Drinking this red house wine makes me think of a big warm hug from Buck. No sex, just cuddle. Will he be at Ole's funeral on Saturday?

—Suddenly Lonely Lena

Buck's house wine is distributed in the United States by U-Haul and Brothers.

When I was just a little grape,

I asked my mother, "What will I be?

Will I be pretty, will I be rich?"

Here's what she said to me.

"Que Syrah, Syrah,

Whatever will be, will be.

The vintage's not ours to see.

Que Syrah, Syrah."

With apologies to Jay Livingston and Ray Evans.

Editor's Note: Buck's house wine has not been reviewed in *Whine Affectionado* or other grape pulp magazines. He refuses to send complimentary cases of his Que Syrah to the wine snots on magazine mastheads, or provide complimentary lodge rooms for their lusty liaisons with Trader Joe's bulk wine buyers.

Offal Things with Recipes

Offal is from the Old French word used to describe English food. The following are listed alphabetically, not in the order of easy removal. Each can be enjoyed individually as an offal snack, as an entrée such as Sonofabitch Stew, or as a Humble Pie just desert.

Brains

Left brain or right brain? When you look at an animal's brain, you will find no evidence of advanced thought, actually no thought at all. Like ours, their left lobe controls reasoning and language. If, for example, you smack a deer hard on the left side of its head, the animal is unable to divide or subtract. If you smack him hard stage right, the deer loses key senses and its ability to watercolor or arrange forest flowers. The brain of a large game animal is most likely larger than your boss's gray matter and certainly tastier.

Fixing brains is a no-brainer. Soak a lobe in cold water for several hours, changing water often until clean. In a 3-quart pot, add fresh water, several onion quarters, a sliced clove of garlic, and a pinch of salt, and bring to a boil. Remove the lobe, let cool, and slice into small 1-inch "steaks." When hungry, roll the slices in flour or panko, dip in an egg, and fry in a skillet over medium heat for 3 to 4 minutes per side.

Caution: Do not eat squirrel brains from in and around Kentucky, as the animals may carry a squirrelly version of mad cow disease that is transmitted and fatal to humans. The relationship between mad cows and mad squirrels isn't clear, but you can be sure any contact was after hours, under a moonless sky, long after the mad scientist's bedtime. Those who do not die of the disease display unusual behaviors such as trying to crawl into a hole in an old red oak tree and burying nuts in the backyard.

Chitlins

Short for *chitterlings*, hog or pig intestines hang lower than testicles on the free wild game chart, but once cleaned, boiled for several hours, cut into strips, and allowed to cool before eating with a dip or rolled in flour, deep-fried, and served hot, you still won't ask for seconds. Bachelor farmers in northern Minnesota say it smells like bad lutefisk. Professional football players say it smells like preseason locker room.

For the bird brainiacs: Upland bird intestines, carefully cleaned, cut into small pieces, fried slowly in butter and olive oil, and folded into whipped eggs make a great omelet.

Pig ears are high fashion in young top chefs' kitchens—boiled for a day and a half, cut into thin strips, and deep-fried . . . and mixed with every taste and texture you can imagine.

Eggs

It's very unlikely an egg will be intact following a bird-bumper inter-action. Best used in the upland bird intestine omelet (see above).

Face

"Losing face" has little resonance in the wild game world and there are food adventurers who have eaten face; pig face, that is. Those that eat face eat pig ears, too. They experience umami in their individual hog heavens.

Gizzards

These are secondary stomachs in birds and used to grind their food before digestion. If birds had teeth, deep-fried gizzards available at ser-vice station food marts would disappear, much to many road warriors' and construction workers' dismay.

Wash gizzards and cover with salt, ground black pepper, and garlic powder. Roll in flour and deep-fry until done. Serve with your favorite sauce, such as Buck's preferred dip of honey mustard and creamy horse-radish. Your dentist recommends overcooked gizzards.

Hands

Only Disney animals have hands. Mother Nature's wards have paws and the known pause for the cause is the soft mitt of a large bear. However, a large bear is not anxious for an involuntary handout.

Head

When you boil the head of any animal in salted water, cover the head with a towel or, if a small mammal, a Shriner's cap, to keep it light colored. Slow-cooking for an hour should just about do it. Remove face meats, trim, and serve with dipping sauces. A heads-up: This may not be appropriate for polite company.

For the holidays: Animal skulls have long been used in cult activities and Halloween provides the perfect opportunity for a roadside shopper to showcase a collection of skulls, especially when flanking a specially carved pumpkin.

Heart

I ♥ Buck. A deer camp favorite, fresh deer heart is a first-night-in-camp weekend special. Very little preparation is involved as deer hearts are usually broken from a new understanding of how cruel is their world. Trim the hard end, slice into 1-inch steaks, and fix like liver.

Headcheese

The most likely place you'll find cheese in or on a head is at a Green Bay Packers game. Headcheese is head meat and often called "souse," which is an indication of the blood alcohol level of those who enjoy it. Slowly simmer the head meat (including cheeks, lips, eyebrows, and dimples), and once cool, the natural gelatin in the skull congeals into aspic, which can then be sliced for sandwiches. Bachelor farmers around Buck's lodge in northern Minnesota call it "sulte," and make darn sure meatballs are also available at the church suppers.

Kidneys

For many, steak and kidney pie is one of the main reasons the Brits lost their empire. Animal kidneys are prepared like livers and gizzards and used with forest mushrooms in a musty kebab. Remember—these kidneys perform the same function as yours. Num, num.

Liver

Fresh liver pan-fried in butter and covered with sautéed white onions is a road-shopper's Blue Plate Special.

Bird liver is softer than gizzard. Trim and rinse the liver, then soak in buttermilk for 15 minutes and drain. Dredge the liver in seasoned flour until completely coated. Dip again in buttermilk and dust once more for a double coating. Fry in hot oil for several minutes and turn only once. Drain on paper towels and season with salt. Serve hot.

Ignore the implications of the question, "What am I—chopped liver?" This is another taste treat that goes well with chopped onion and hard-boiled egg. A New York deli serving suggestion: on top of a cup of chilled, chopped iceberg lettuce.

Marrow (Bone)

Prairie butter, the marrow from buffalo femurs, was the Smuckers® of early mountain men. The leg bones are cut into sections, boiled, and split lengthwise for dipping with your bowie knife. Spread on sourdough bread.

Neck

Bird necks are best used as flavoring ingredients in stew. Large animal neck meat is best used in stews or ground round. As noted earlier, horse neck meat can be a mane dish for high-stepping carnivores.

Nose

The Great White North has shown culinary interest in the soft nose of the moose. Preparations are sketchy and often written on the inside of a piece of birch or poplar bark, but it seems all you need to do is boil the snot out of it.

Pork Rind

Deep-fried pork skin is high in protein, but the rinds in a convenience store replace this with high sodium content. Homemade cracklings are easy to make and the best are pheasant skin deep-fried in peanut oil and served hot.

Sweetbreads

Sweetbread comes from the Old English *sweete braed.* The thymus and pancreas glands of large animals are rarely recognized on the road, as most shoppers don't know where they are located. The appropriate preparation is best described as "soft": sauté slowly in garlic-infused extra-virgin olive oil and mild onions. Serve hot.

Tail

The "pope's nose," or turkey tail, has a sliver of meat encased in the fat. When that part of the bird is your main meal source, you've reached the tail end of your supper. Beaver tails are held over an open fire to soften the fat for easy peeling, rolled in seasoned flour, and fried in extra-virgin olive oil. Keep the double entendre jokes to yourself. Buck's Aussie friends say kangaroo tail is worth the effort, but keep in mind Australians lead the world in per capita beer consumption.

Testicles

Prairie oysters, or lamb fries, are usually from a local source and are a novel food often promoted at fund-raisers. Look closely at the event photos—only men and a few scorned women seem to enjoy this culinary adventure. The donors' eyes remain crossed. See Testicle Festival (page 87).

Tongue

Tongue is a tough muscle, especially in animals low on the food chain that stick their tongues out at slow predators. For finger-lickin' mouth meat, boil a large animal's tongue in salted water for an hour, drain, and peel the skin. Change the water and add ½ cup of diced onion, 1 chopped stalk of celery, 6 bay leaves, 12 peppercorns, and 1 tablespoon of red wine. Bring to a boil, lower to a simmer, and cook for 4 hours. Let cool, slice, and serve with hot mustard or horseradish dip.

Tripe

The inner lining of large ruminants' stomachs has long lined the stomachs of large European (royal and nonroyal) human ruminants. The Quick-Fix recipe is simple: Boil the tripe until tender, and cut into 1-inch squares. In a skillet, brown ½ cup each of minced onion and celery in extra-virgin olive oil and add 6 ounces of dry red wine. Add the tripe and simmer for 1 hour. In another skillet, warm ¼ cup of extra-virgin olive oil and 1 minced garlic clove. Add to the tripe mixture and cook for a few minutes before serving.

Udders

See Chitlins. In inexperienced hands, cooking these can be an udder disaster.

Disclaimers in All
North American Languages

1. Eating game meat on an irregular basis can cause temporary acute gastric distress, especially troubling for those in adjoining office cubicles and the elevator. Tell the troubled it's cancer related.

2. Black tarry stools are associated with wild game meat diets, especially for those who live on bear meat. The stools need at least two flushes in the new water-saving toilets or an extra layer of lime in the outdoor biffy.

3. A shopper's first wild game meal will help cure acute constipation. Within twenty-four hours after your Shish Kaboom Kebabs (page 62), you'll "drop the kids off at the pool" at least once.

4. There are risks associated with eating undercooked game meat, as is the case with other raw protein products. If you suffer from chronic office fatigue syndrome, immune system deficiencies such as metrosexualism, and honesty deficiencies endemic to those who seek and occupy political offices, all game products should be fully cooked.

Buck's Quick Tip: Don't smoke cigarettes while preparing road groceries. Smoking is not good for you. And it's disrespectful to the animal that never had a chance to savor a good cigar with you on the back deck.

Bucket List: One Hundred Animals to Run Over Before You Eat a Dirt Sandwich

Amphibians (turtles, lizards, snakes, alligators, and crocodiles) ✓[2]

Antelope ✓ ✓ ✓ ✓ ✓ ✓ ✓ ✓ ✓ ✓

Armadillo ✓ ✓ ✓ ✓ ✓ ✓ ✓

Bear, Black ✓

Bear, Brown ✓

Bear, Polar (snowmobile shopping cart) **TBA**

Beaver ✓

Buffalo (Yellowstone National Park after closing) ✓

Caribou ✓

Deer, Blacktail ✓

Deer, Coues (Southwest) ✓

Deer, Key (Florida) ✓

Deer, Mule ✓ ✓ ✓

Deer, Sitka (Alaska) ✓ ✓ ✓

Deer, Whitetail ✓ ✓ ✓ ✓ ✓ ✓ ✓ ✓ ✓ ✓ ✓ ✓ ✓ ✓

Elk, Rocky Mountain ✓

Elk, Roosevelt ✓

Hare ✓ ✓ ✓ ✓ ✓ ✓

Moose ✓

Muskrat ✓

Otter ✓

Pheasant ✓ ✓ ✓ ✓ ✓ ✓ ✓ ✓ ✓

Porcupine ✓

Possum ✓ ✓ ✓ ✓ ✓ ✓ ✓ ✓ ✓ ✓ ✓ ✓ ✓ ✓ ✓ ✓

Quail, California ✓

Quail, Gambel's ✓ ✓ ✓ ✓ ✓ ✓

Quail, Montezuma's ✓

Quail, Mountain ✓

Quail, Northern Bobwhite ✓

Quail, Scaled ✓

Rabbit ✓ ✓ ✓ ✓ ✓ ✓

Raccoon ✓ ✓ ✓ ✓ ✓ ✓

Reptiles (salamanders, frogs, and toads) ✓ ✓ ✓ ✓ ✓ ✓ ✓ ✓ ✓

Sheep ✓

Squirrel, Eastern and Western Gray ✓ ✓ ✓ ✓ ✓ ✓ ✓ ✓ ✓ ✓

Squirrel, Fox ✓

Squirrel, Ground (56 species, including prairie dogs, chipmunks, and, wearing crimson and yellow, the Minnesota Gophers) ✓ ✓ ✓ ✓

Squirrel, Northern and Southern Flying ✓

Turkey, Eastern ✓ ✓ ✓ ✓ ✓ ✓

Turkey, farmer's wife's pet gobbler (more likely) ✓

Turkey, Gould's ✓

Turkey, Merriam's ✓

Turkey, Ocellated (unlikely)

Turkey, Osceola ✓

Turkey, Rio Grande ✓

Underdogs (fox, coyotes, and wolves) ✓

Wolverine (unlikely)

Roadkill Chefs'
Best Cooking Secrets

Buck talks to several famous roadkill chefs to learn the tricks of their trade.

J. Angus "Sourdough" McLean

Cast-Iron Chef and Carni-Whore

Cleanliness: I wash my hands after skinning an animal. Makes me feel like a raccoon.

Pantry Essentials: Boxer shorts

Equipment: A multitool for removing porcupine quills, a tire pump, and a used army flamethrower

Secret Roadside Cooking Tip: Never use asphalt shingles as a fuel source.

Salvatore Umberto Alighieri Glynn

Cast-Right Iron Dog Shooter and Pantry Boy

Spices: I don't go into any tavern without my special drink spices for the girls.

Equipment: My parole officer says I will get my knives back in November. Like I believe him.

Table Decorations: At home I swear by vinyl tablecloths, the ones with a soft underlayer so it doesn't blow off the table when you hose the top.

Secret Roadside Cooking Tip: Mojito lip balm

Babe Peterson

Buck's First Wife and Overlord of All That Is Cooked

Timing: I serve my food when I'm good and ready. Now leave me the hell alone.

Animals in the Kitchen: No llamas in my kitchen. I'm talking live ones here.

Style: I've always cooked with my left hand. That's where I have all my fingers.

Secret Roadside Divorce Tip: Let sleeping dogs lie, especially if they aren't breathing.

About the Author

Buck Peterson is the Road scholar of game cookery. From the culinary classic, *The Original Road Kill Cookbook*, to the *Totaled Roadkill Cookbook*, his books are the definitive works on the subject, not to mention his creation of a large, fiscally conservative, morally liberal, intellectually keen Buckster audience with his *Endangered Species Cookbook*, *International Roadkill Cookbook*, and *The Roadkill USA Coloring Book*. His work in utilizing roadkill has earned him the executive directorship of the Meals Under Wheels Foundation®, a not-for-profit charity that services the needs of thrifty shoppers of all ages and spiritual persuasions, except Missouri Synod Lutherans who wouldn't let Buck bury his dead horse, Whiney the Poo, in their damn cemetery. Buck was raised in the Midwestern hunting tradition, with wild game as a table staple. From his hunting camp experience near Spider Lake, Minnesota, he founded the Frequent Fryer Club. Join Buck, Sourdough McLean, and Dorothy the Hunting Pig at www. buckpeterson.com. If it takes a little time to find them, they're probably down in the bomb shelter, reloading. Caution: Tiptoe by the door. *Do not* make any loud noises.

Editor's Note: Seriously, don't even knock on the shelter door. We're still missing two Jehovah's Witness missionaries.